FORGIVENESS
IS REALLY STRANGE

Masi Noor & Marina Cantacuzino
Art by Sophie Standing

SINGING
DRAGON

This book is dedicated to all those who have shared their stories and all those who took part in research studies to help illuminate the complex subject of forgiveness.

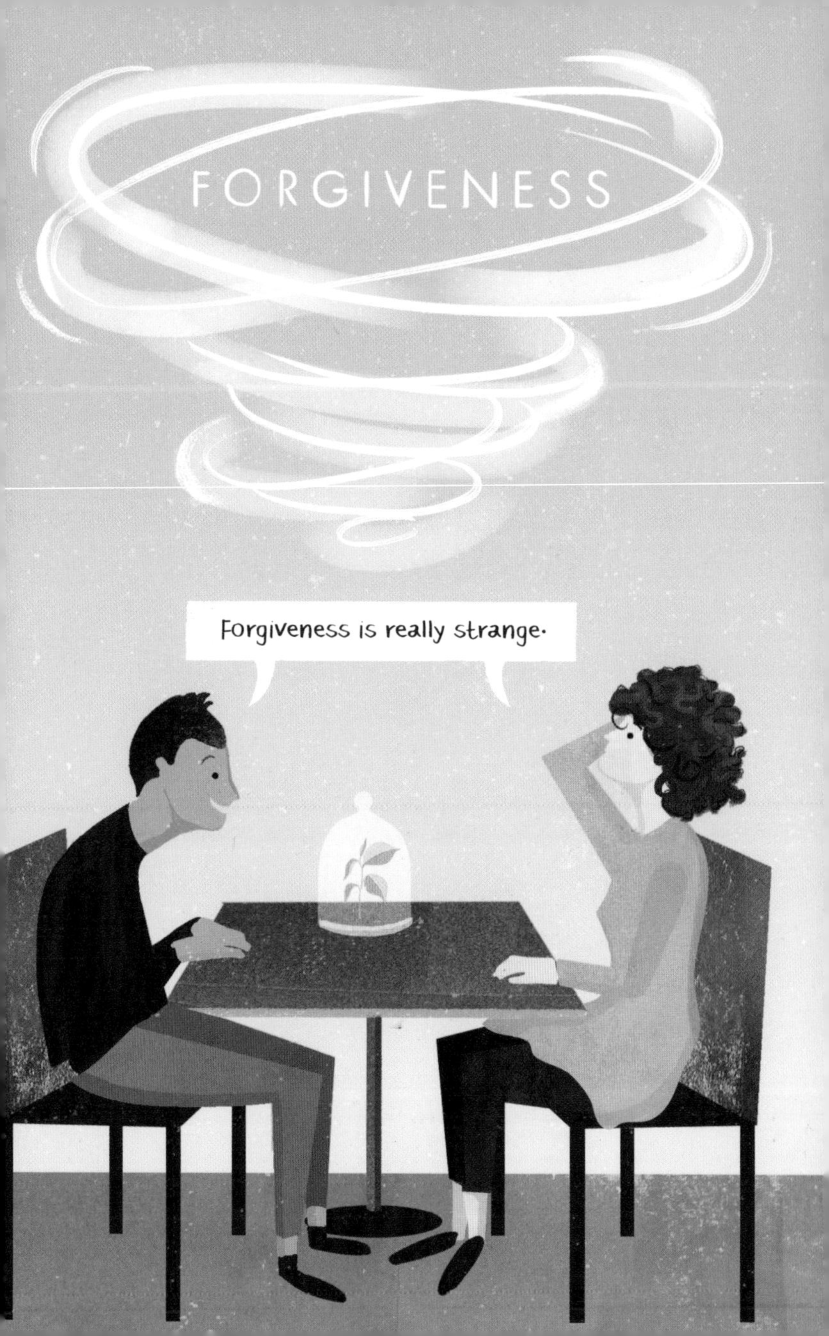
FORGIVENESS
Forgiveness is really strange.

As human beings we are talented thieves.

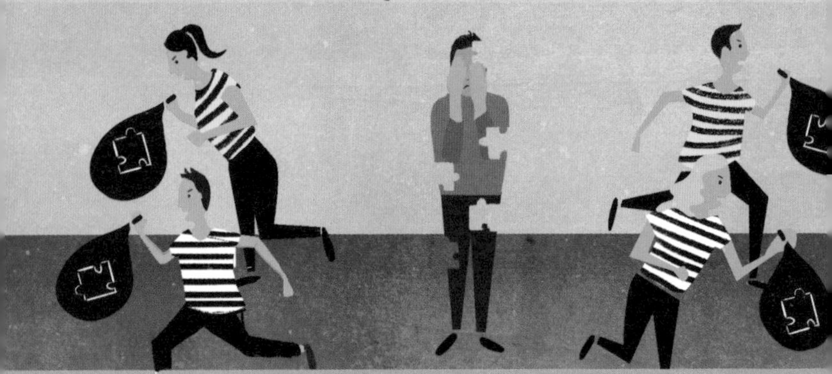

We can rob each other of a loved one, a childhood, a home, a career, dignity, and even an entire future.

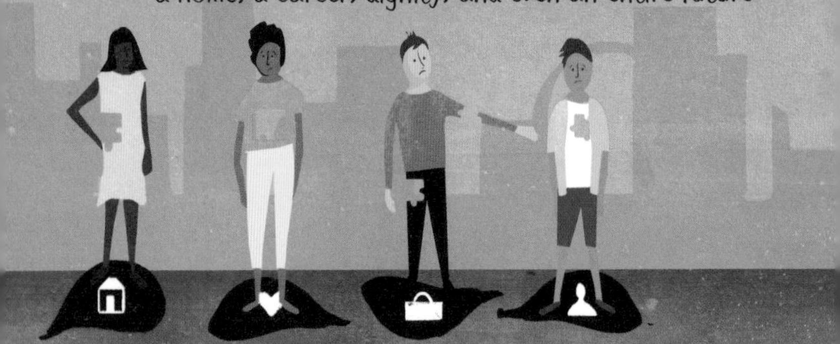

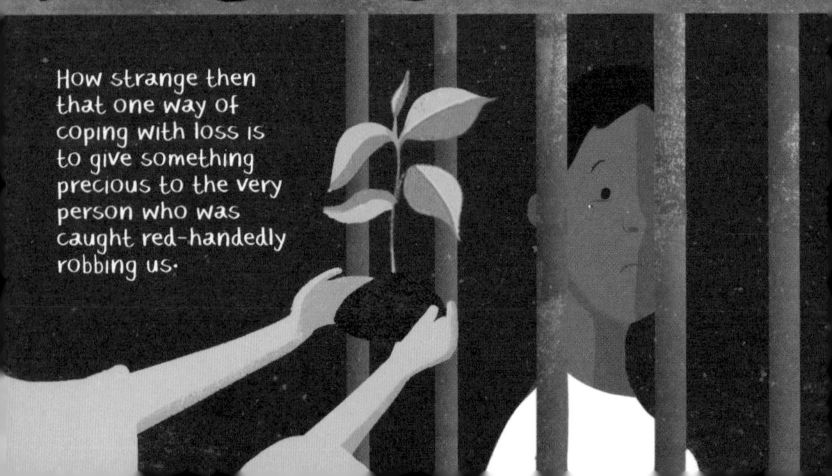
How strange then that one way of coping with loss is to give something precious to the very person who was caught red-handedly robbing us.

In fact, how strange to talk about the 'power' of forgiveness, when the forgiving is done by the weak and the injured.

And why do some victims feel guilt, while perpetrators often don't even feel the need to say sorry?

Would you forgive in order to live longer?

RIP

In this book, we explore all these strange aspects of forgiveness using real-life stories and scientific research.

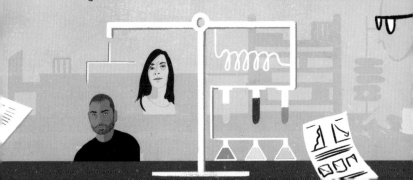

What's your instinctive reaction to being hurt?

Some retreat into silence, like Maya Angelou, who spent 5 years of her childhood not speaking after being sexually abused.

Yet, others become vengeful and devote their entire life to the desire for revenge.

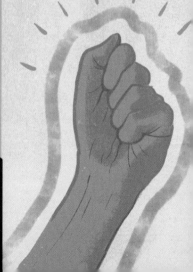

Others use alcohol, drugs or painkillers to numb the pain.

And let's not forget the small, everyday hurts. Like invisible worms, they too can eat away at our peace of mind.

Some are totally immobilized by pain. The writer Richard Holloway notes that the 'shock-waves' reverberating from trauma and injury have the power to bring our lives to a screeching halt.

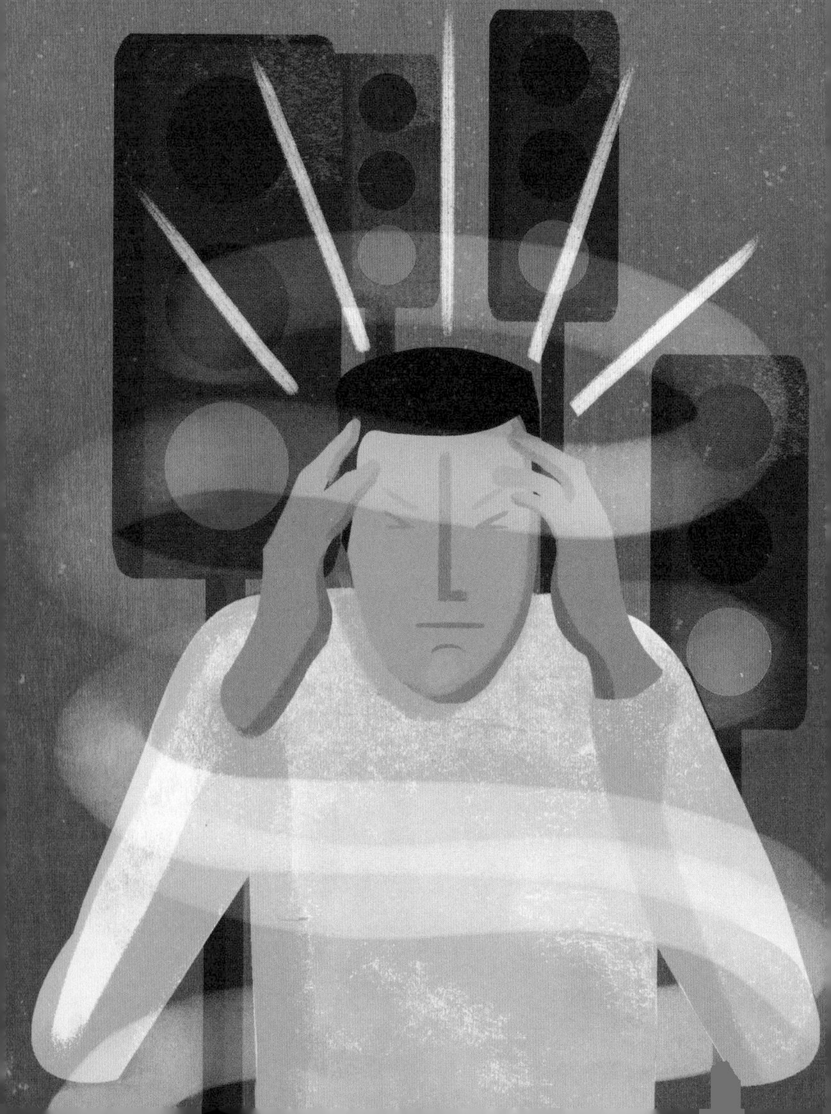

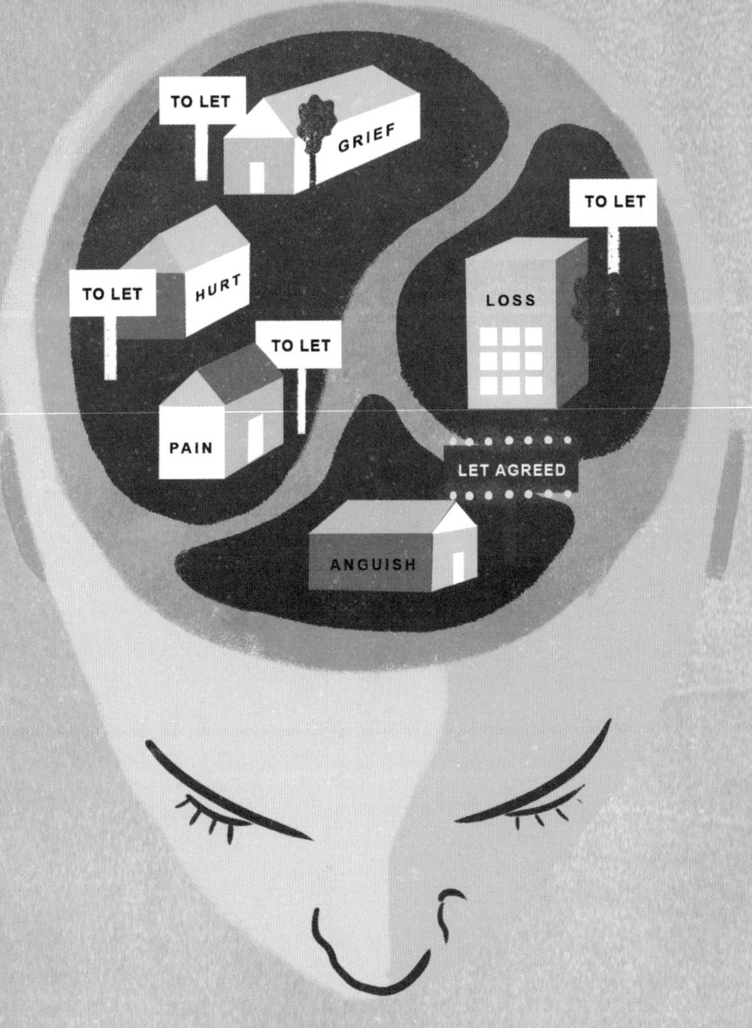
TO LET
GRIEF
TO LET
TO LET
HURT
TO LET
LOSS
PAIN
LET AGREED
ANGUISH

In one way or another, hurts and grievances rule our minds. How much mental space are you willing to rent out to your hurts and grievances?

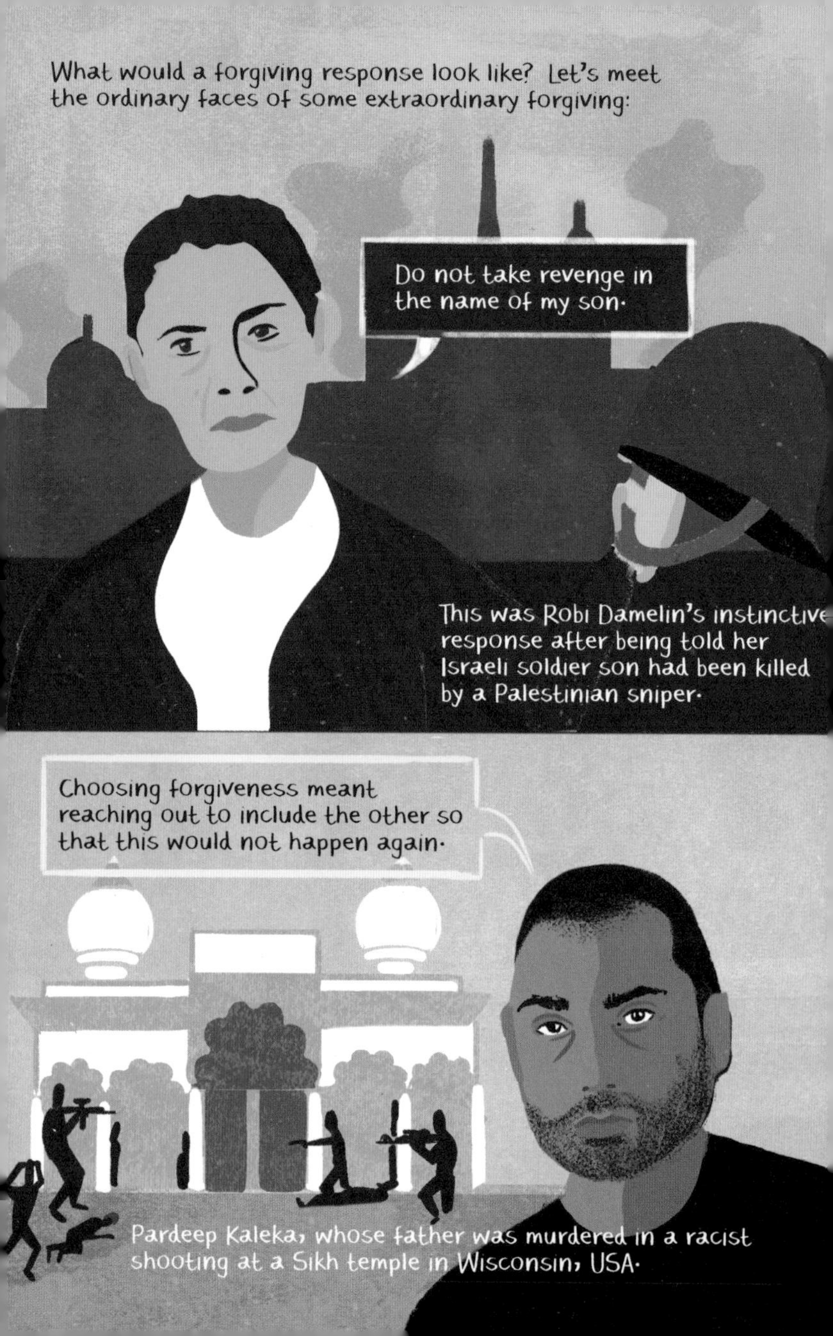
What would a forgiving response look like? Let's meet the ordinary faces of some extraordinary forgiving:
Do not take revenge in the name of my son.
This was Robi Damelin's instinctive response after being told her Israeli soldier son had been killed by a Palestinian sniper.
Choosing forgiveness meant reaching out to include the other so that this would not happen again.
Pardeep Kaleka, whose father was murdered in a racist shooting at a Sikh temple in Wisconsin, USA.

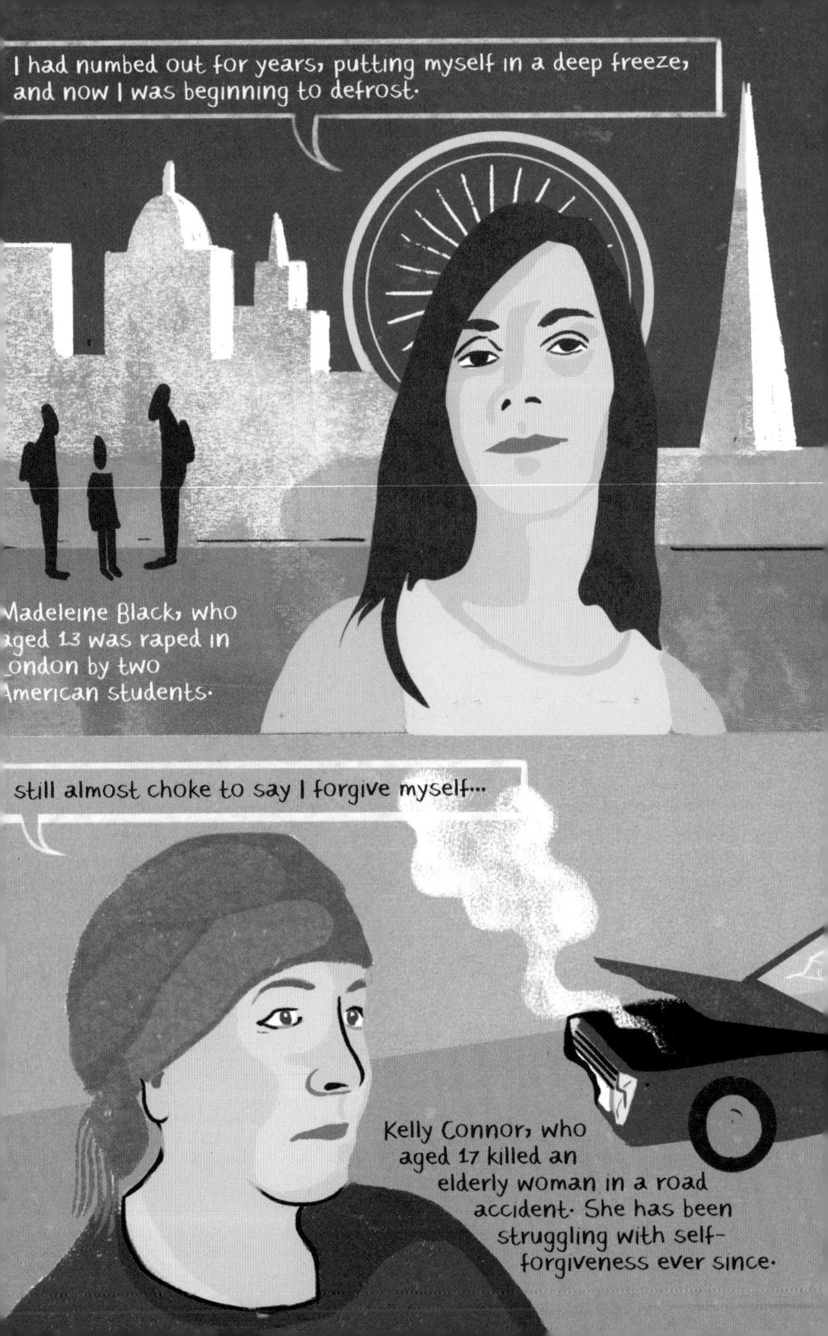
I had numbed out for years, putting myself in a deep freeze, and now I was beginning to defrost.
Madeleine Black, who
aged 13 was raped in
ondon by two
merican students.
still almost choke to say I forgive myself...
Kelly Connor, who aged 17 killed an elderly woman in a road accident. She has been struggling with self-forgiveness ever since.

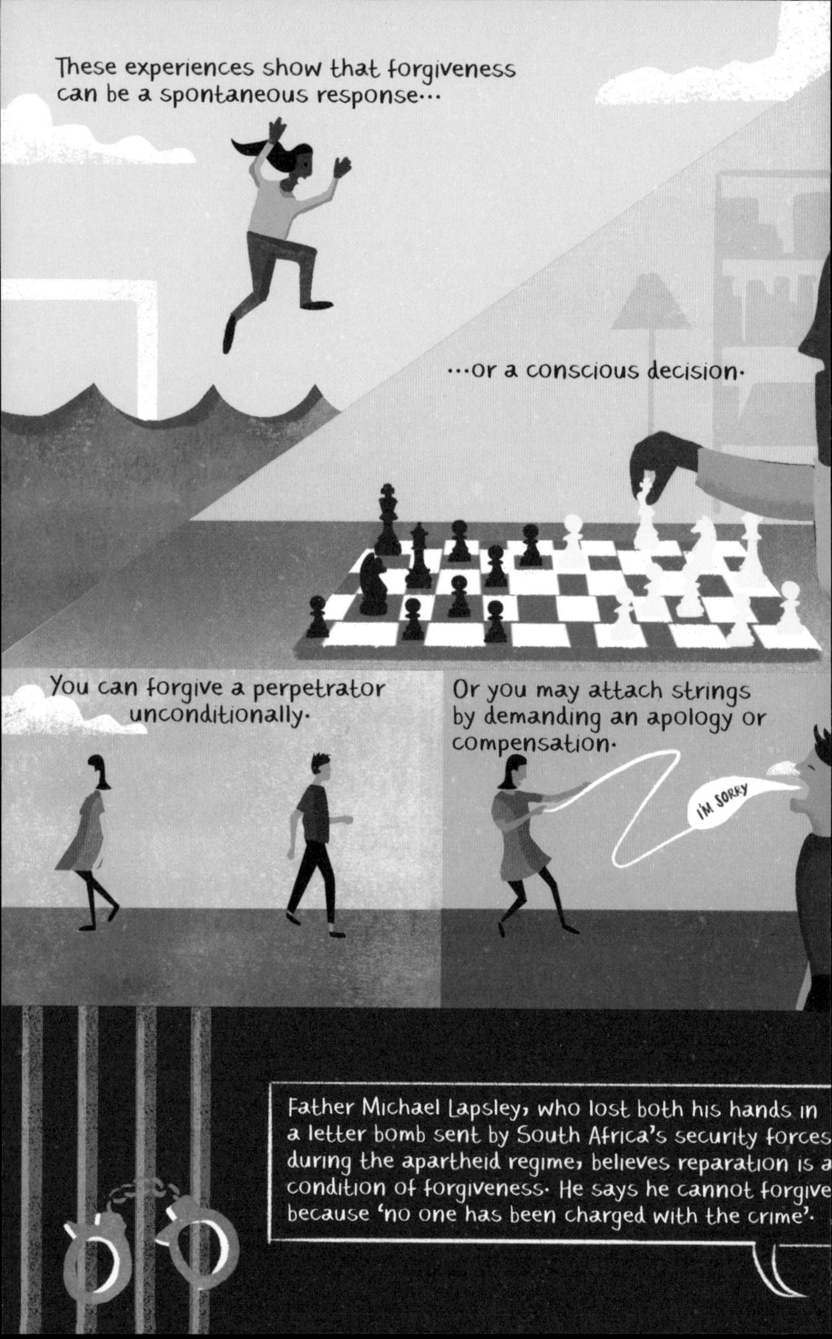
These experiences show that forgiveness can be a spontaneous response...
...or a conscious decision.
You can forgive a perpetrator unconditionally.
Or you may attach strings by demanding an apology or compensation.
I'M SORRY
Father Michael Lapsley, who lost both his hands in a letter bomb sent by South Africa's security forces during the apartheid regime, believes reparation is a condition of forgiveness. He says he cannot forgive because 'no one has been charged with the crime'.

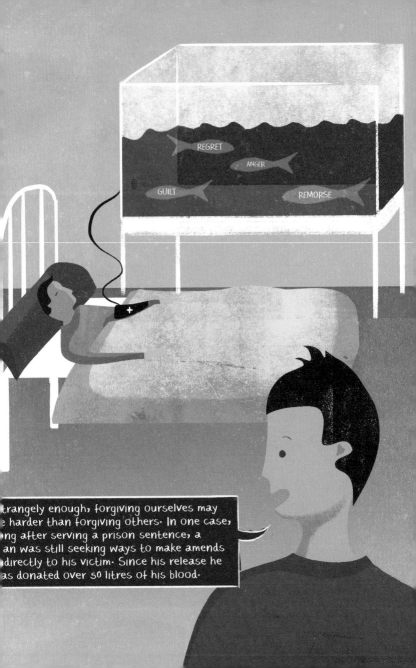

Strangely enough, forgiving ourselves may be harder than forgiving others. In one case, long after serving a prison sentence, a man was still seeking ways to make amends directly to his victim. Since his release he has donated over 50 litres of his blood.

Thus, forgiveness comes in many forms and can sometimes feel quite slippery. The American novelist Mark Twain compares it to 'the fragrance that the violet sheds on the heel that has crushed it'.

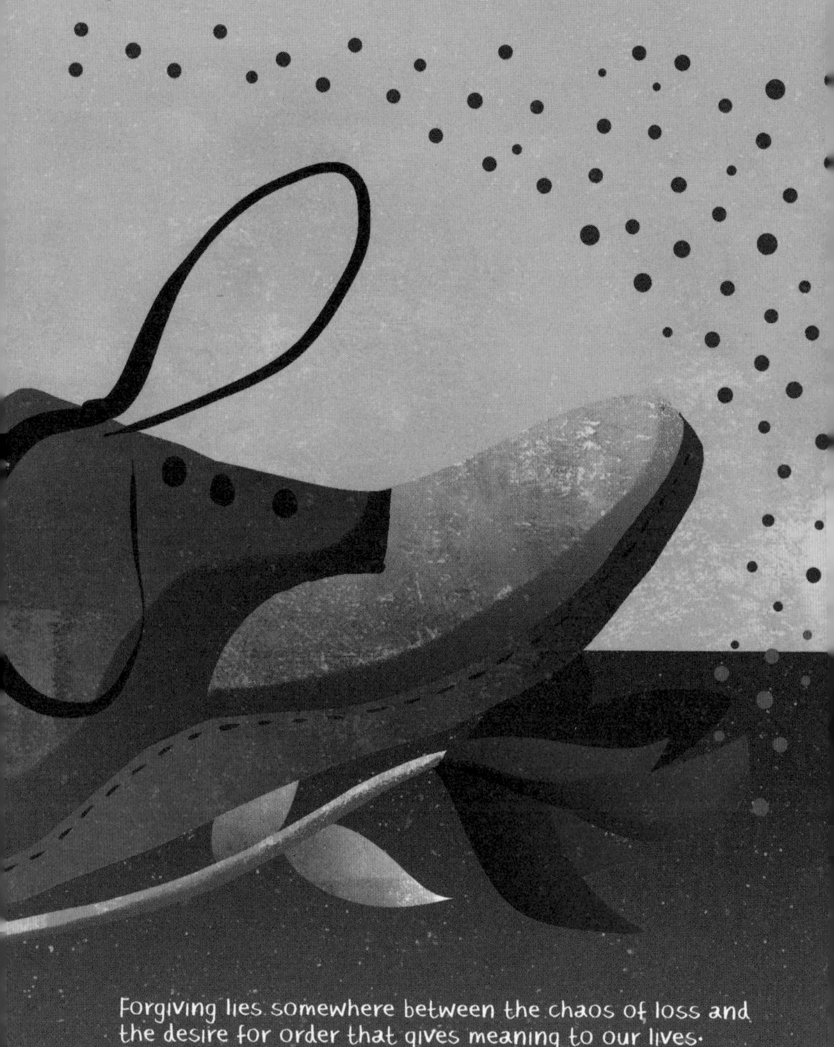

Forgiving lies somewhere between the chaos of loss and the desire for order that gives meaning to our lives.

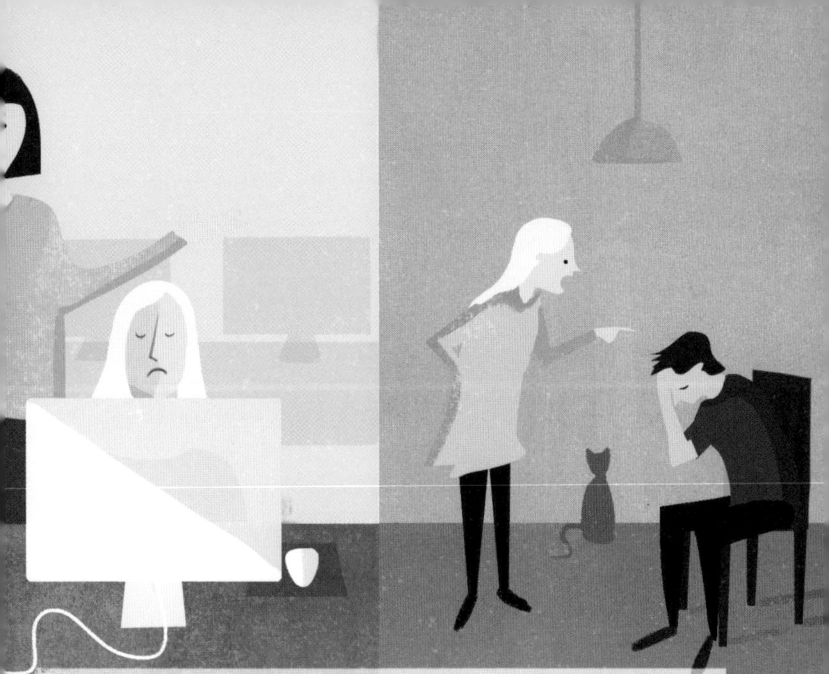

Forgiveness can be used to break the cycle of revenge, as it prevents survivors from using their victimhood to victimize others.

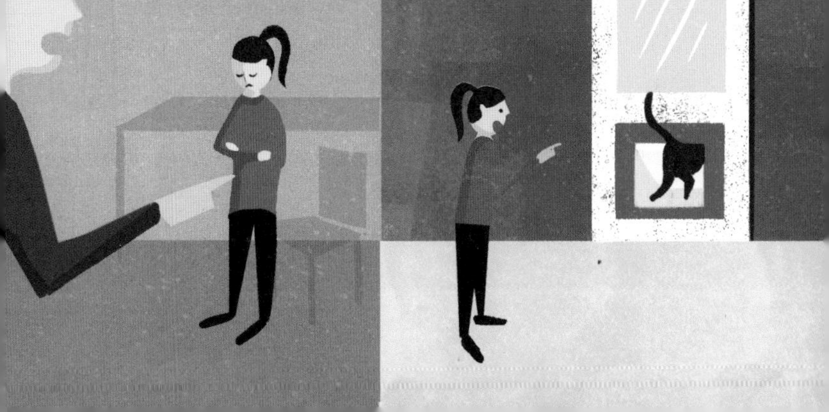

Not everyone approves of forgiving. It cuts public opinion down the middle like a guillotine. There are those who are inspired by it and those who feel morally outraged.

'For those inspired, there is no future for humanity without forgiveness' (D. Tutu).

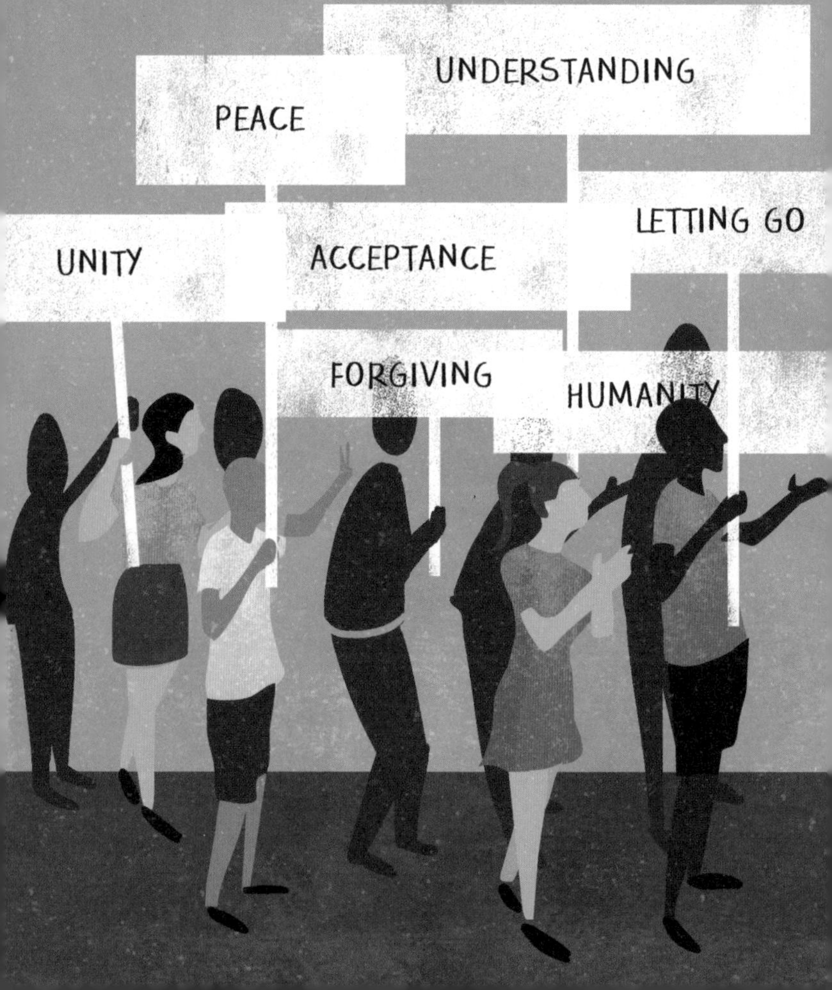
UNDERSTANDING
PEACE
LETTING GO
UNITY
ACCEPTANCE
FORGIVING
HUMANITY

For those outraged, forgiveness is a slap in the face, a licence to hurt. For them, revenge is what really teaches humanity the hard lessons.

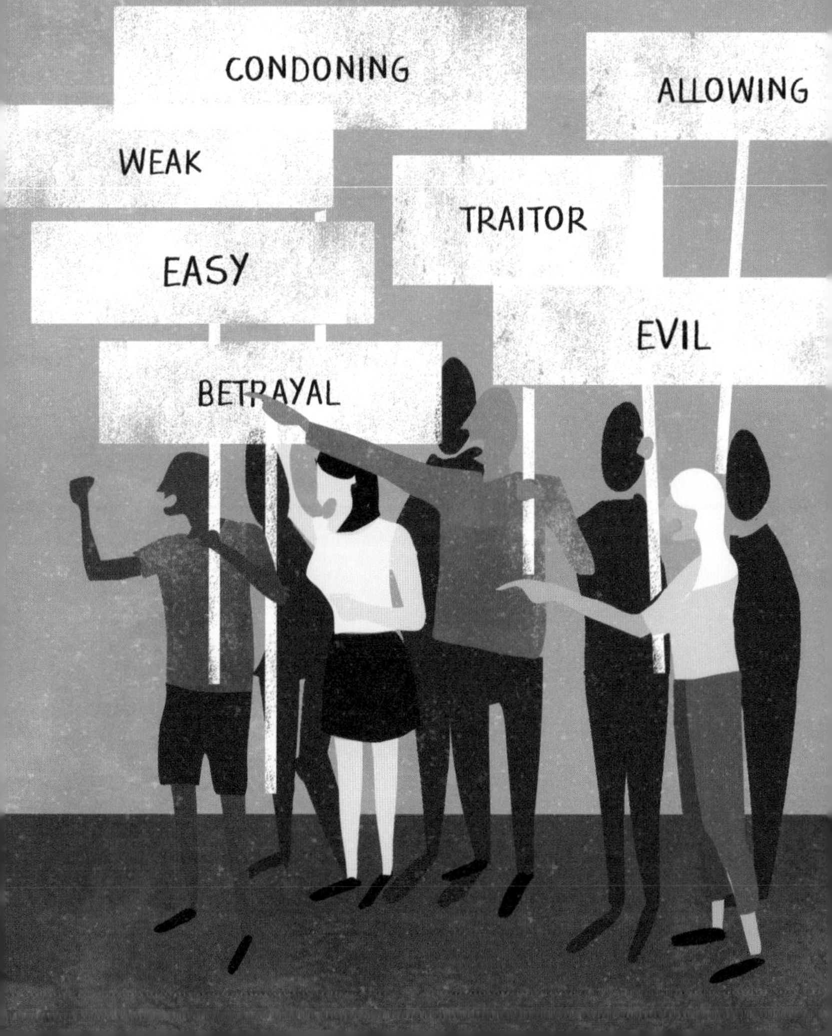
CONDONING
ALLOWING
WEAK
TRAITOR
EASY
EVIL
BETRAYAL

Moral outrage is a very personal thing. From the list below, what would you find most upsetting?

If someone were to...

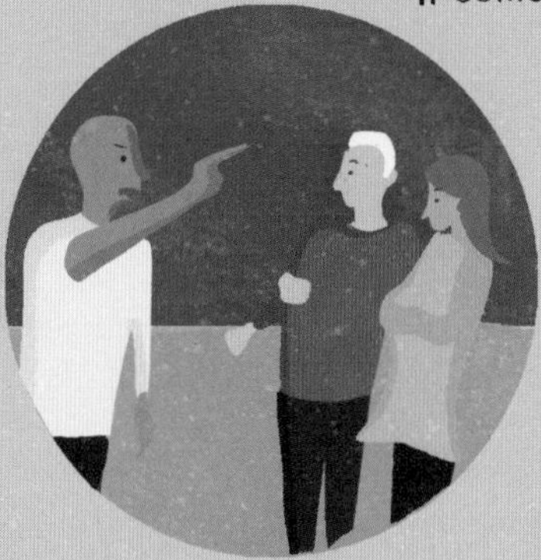

Insult your parents

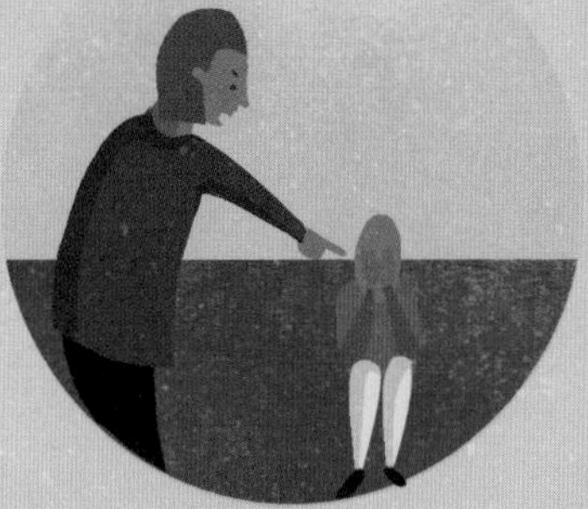

Bully you

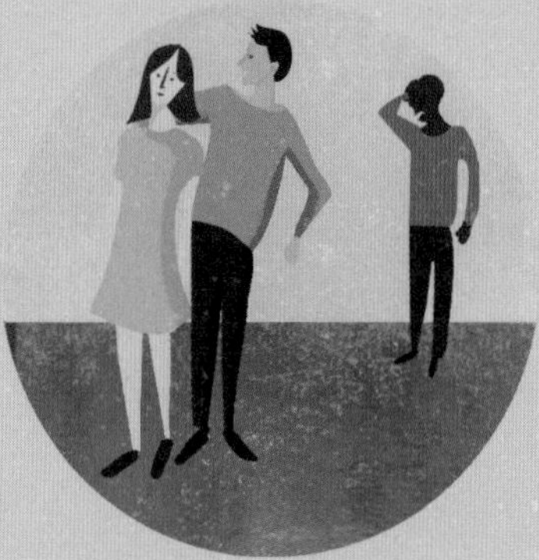

Have a fling with your partner

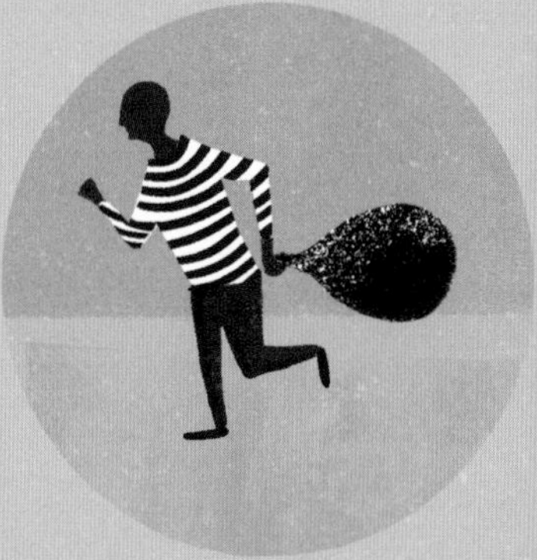

Steal something precious from you

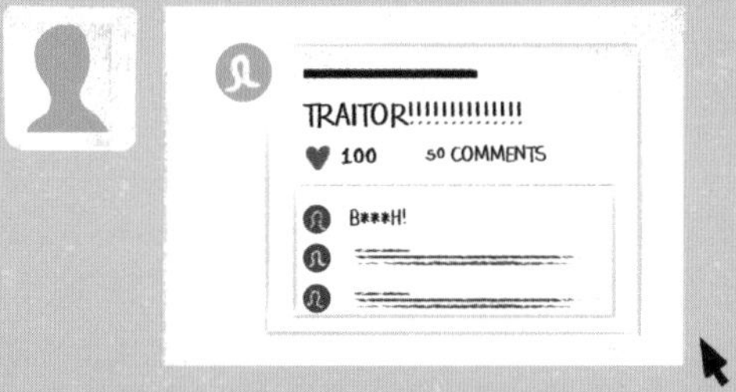
TRAITOR!!!!!!!!!!!!
100
50 COMMENTS
B***H!

Post hate messages about you all over social media

You'll find that different people pick different answers.

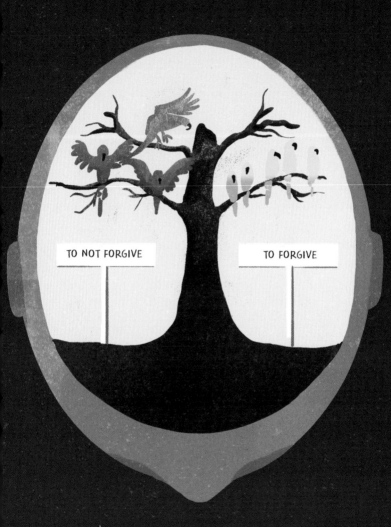

TO NOT FORGIVE

TO FORGIVE

In fact, the tendency to forgive is a bit like a personality trait.
It develops as a result of our upbringing, and how our parents,
teachers and other role models dealt with conflict and hurt.

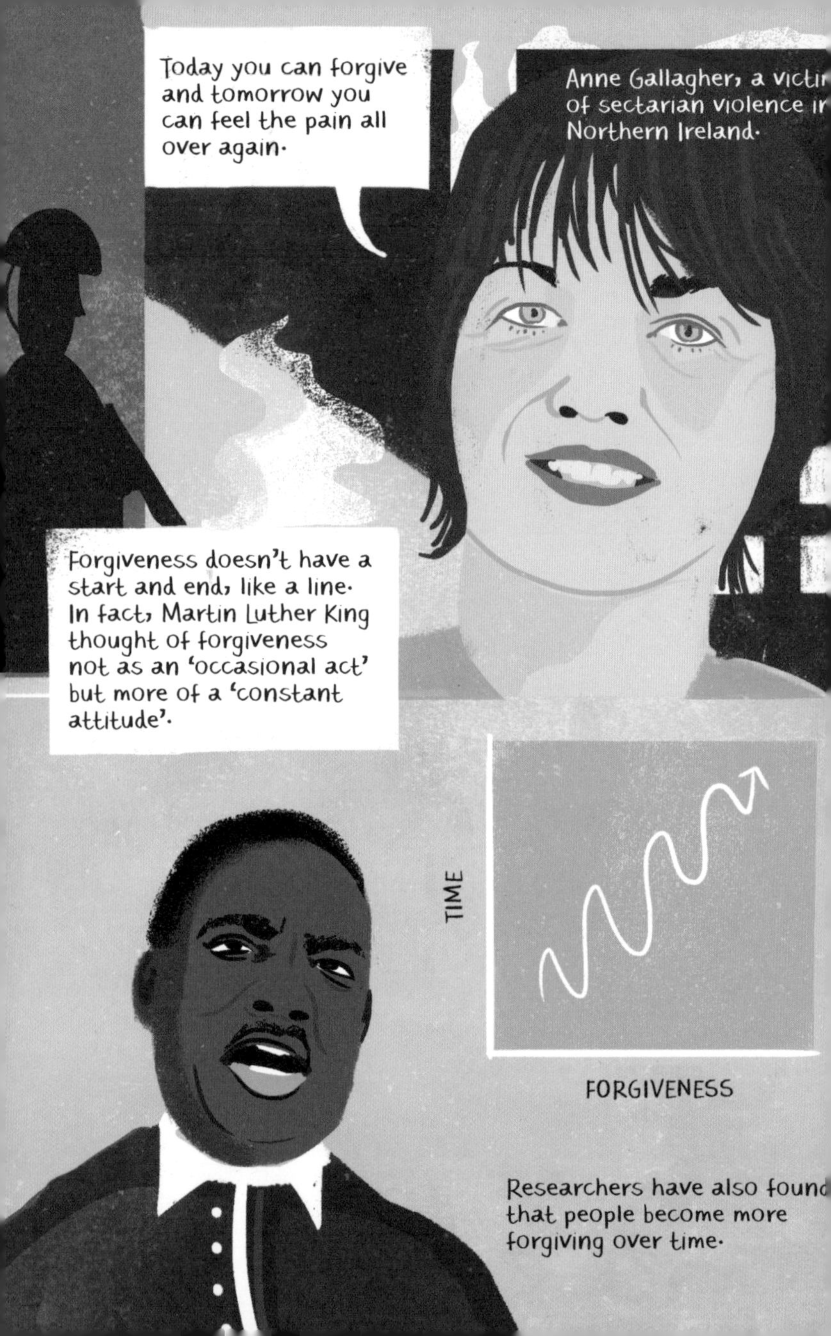
Today you can forgive and tomorrow you can feel the pain all over again.
Anne Gallagher, a victi of sectarian violence i Northern Ireland.
Forgiveness doesn't have a start and end, like a line. In fact, Martin Luther King thought of forgiveness not as an 'occasional act' but more of a 'constant attitude'.
TIME
FORGIVENESS
Researchers have also foun that people become more forgiving over time.

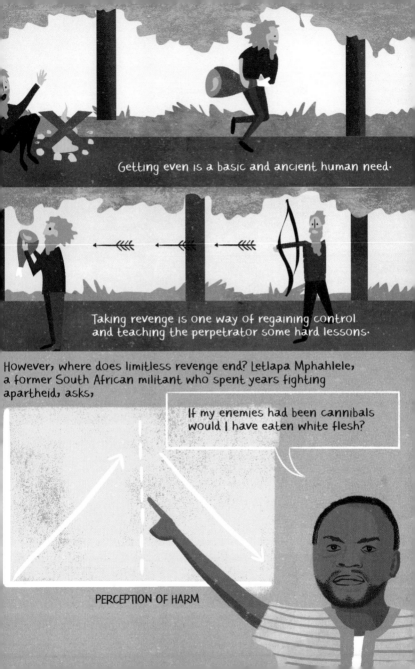

Getting even is a basic and ancient human need.

Taking revenge is one way of regaining control and teaching the perpetrator some hard lessons.

However, where does limitless revenge end? Letlapa Mphahlele, a former South African militant who spent years fighting apartheid, asks,

If my enemies had been cannibals would I have eaten white flesh?

PERCEPTION OF HARM

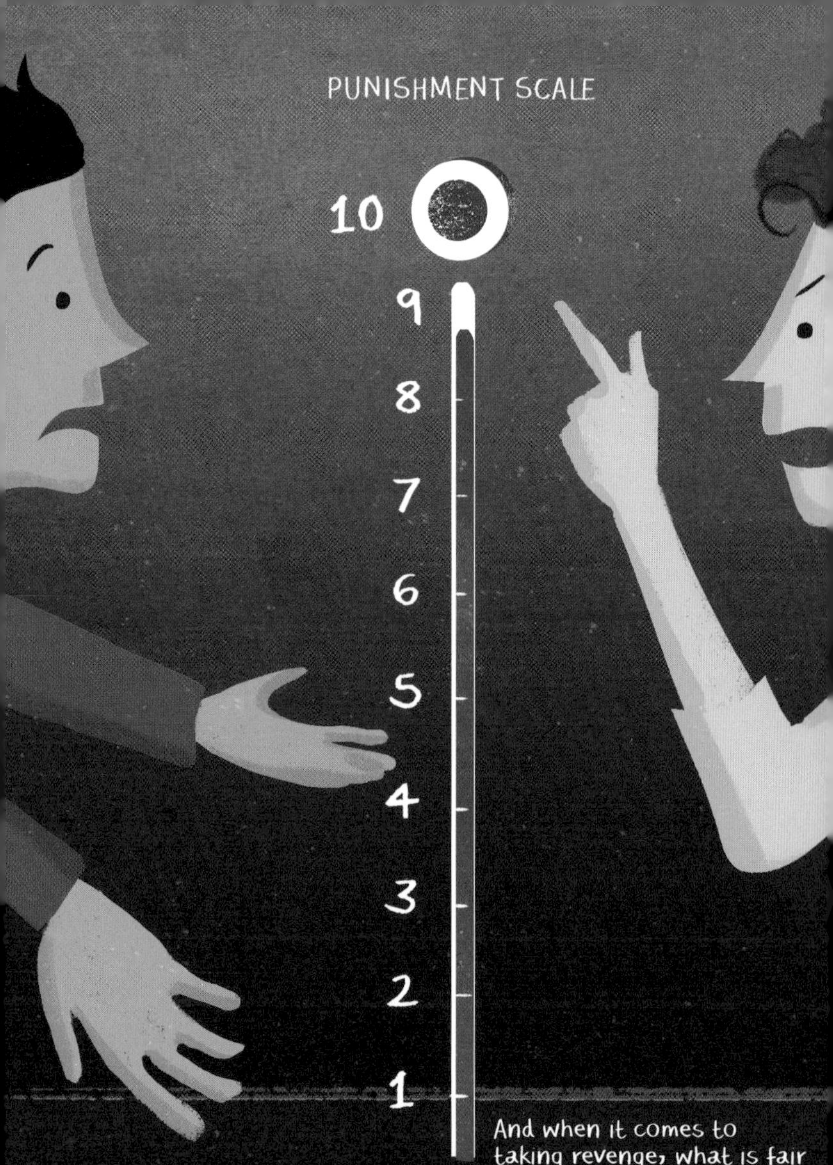
PUNISHMENT SCALE
10
9
8
7
6
5
4
3
2
1

And when it comes to taking revenge, what is fair punishment? Rarely will victim and perpetrators agree. This is why revenge usually leads to yet more hurt and damage.

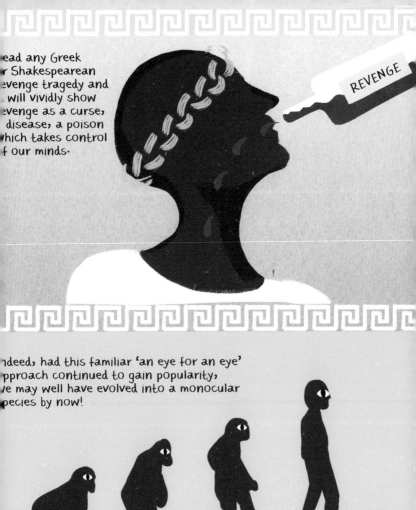

ead any Greek r Shakespearean evenge tragedy and will vividly show evenge as a curse, disease, a poison hich takes control f our minds.

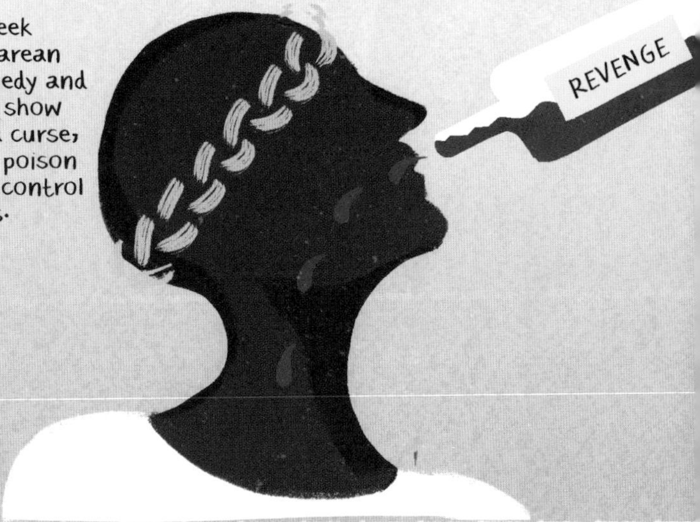
REVENGE

ndeed, had this familiar 'an eye for an eye' pproach continued to gain popularity, e may well have evolved into a monocular pecies by now!

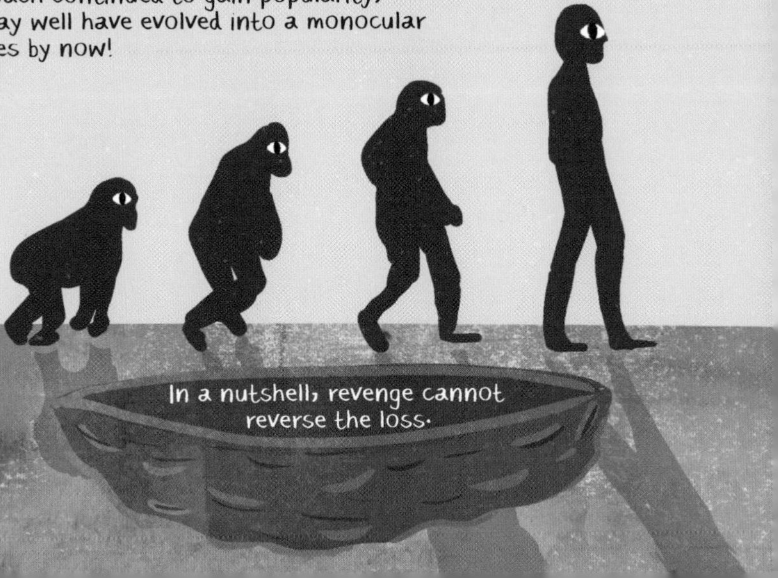

In a nutshell, revenge cannot reverse the loss.

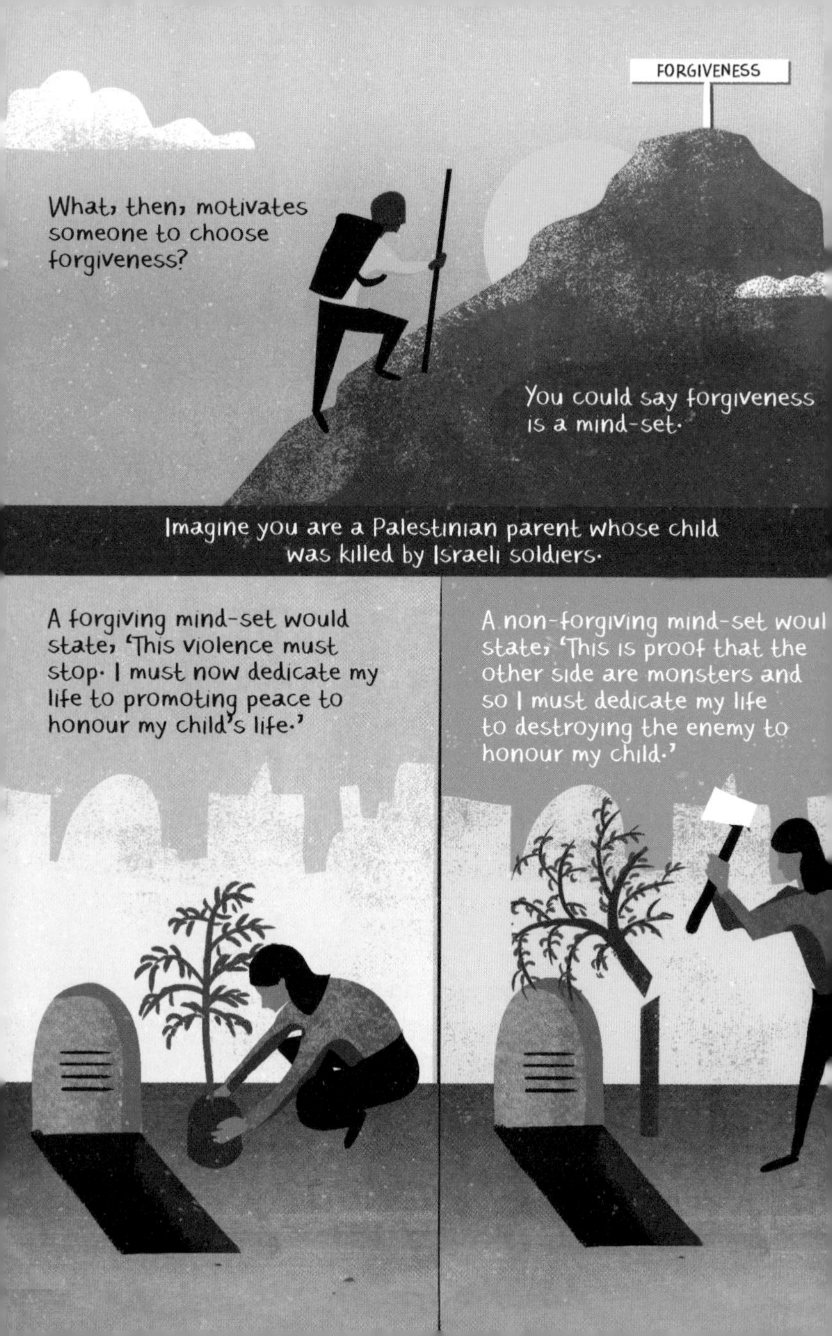
FORGIVENESS
What, then, motivates someone to choose forgiveness?
You could say forgiveness is a mind-set.
Imagine you are a Palestinian parent whose child was killed by Israeli soldiers.
A forgiving mind-set would state, 'This violence must stop. I must now dedicate my life to promoting peace to honour my child's life.'
A non-forgiving mind-set woul state, 'This is proof that the other side are monsters and so I must dedicate my life to destroying the enemy to honour my child.'

ther times, victims feel their relationship to the wrongdoer is more
nportant than the injury itself. Instead of taking revenge, they talk
through.

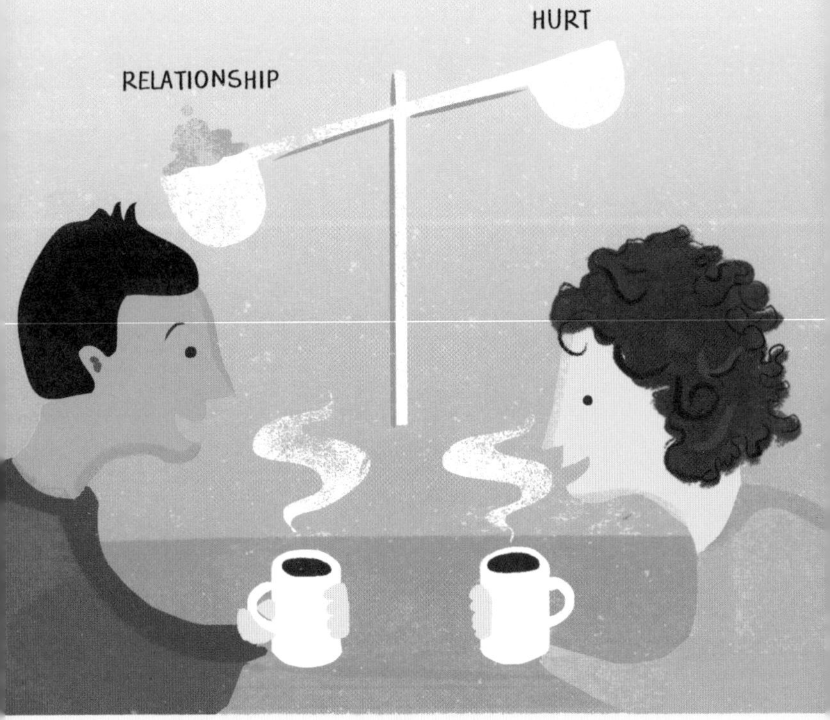
HURT
RELATIONSHIP

In large-scale conflicts, victims may wish to forgive to spare others, including the next generation, the tragic losses they personally experienced.

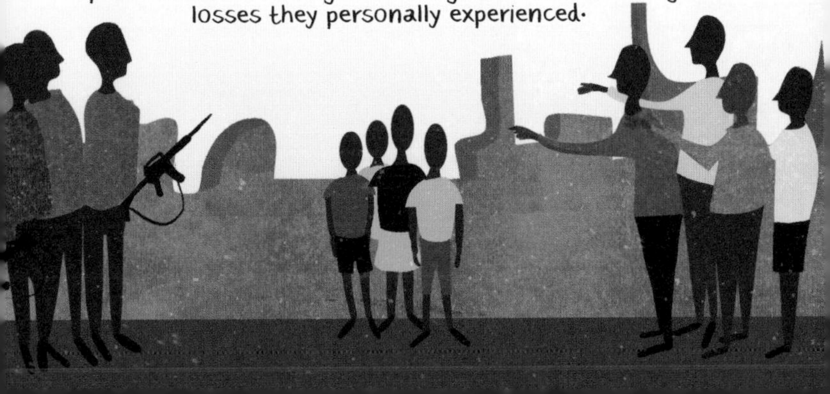

Hurt weakens our sense of control.

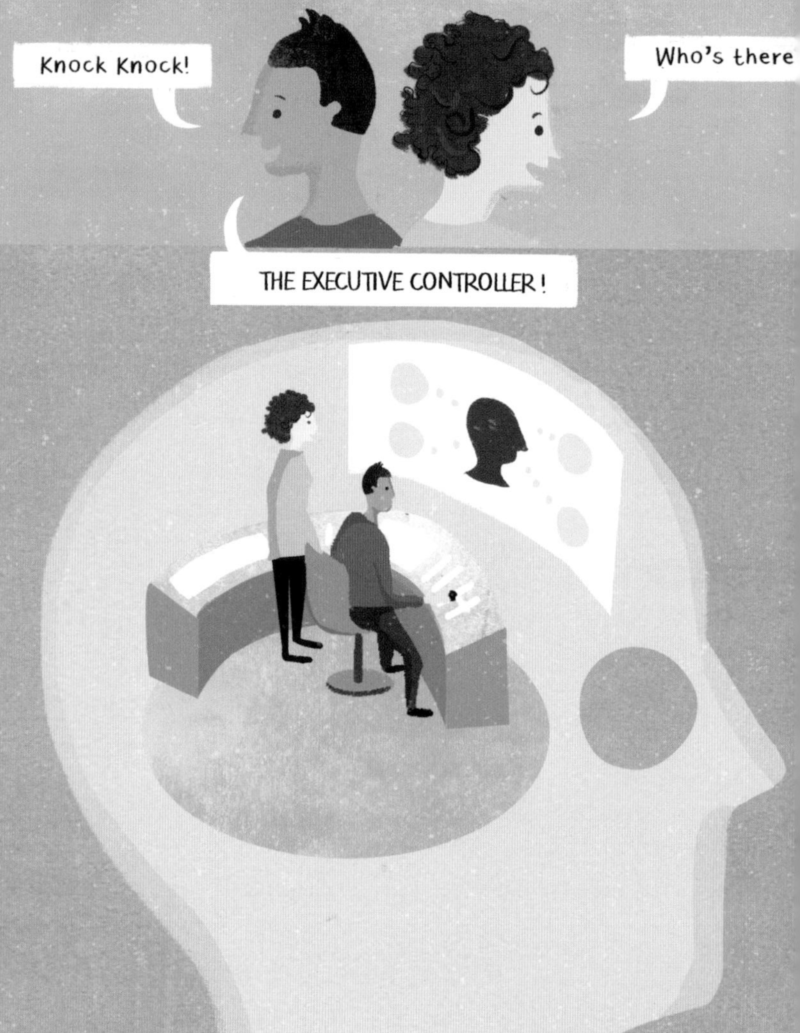
Knock Knock!
Who's there
THE EXECUTIVE CONTROLLER!

Scientists have discovered that our ability to establish control partly lies within our brain's executive functioning system (EFS), which helps us to plan, solve problems and control our thoughts, feelings and behaviours.

searchers have established that the better an individual's EFS works the more likely they are to forgive. We rely on our EFS to reign resentment, or (to use a technical term) 'down-regulate' intrusive oughts such as vengeful fantasies and obsessions.

n index of how well your EFS works is the Stroop task. To do well, ou need the ability to suppress distractions and to focus. Both skills re key to forgiveness, yet very challenging.

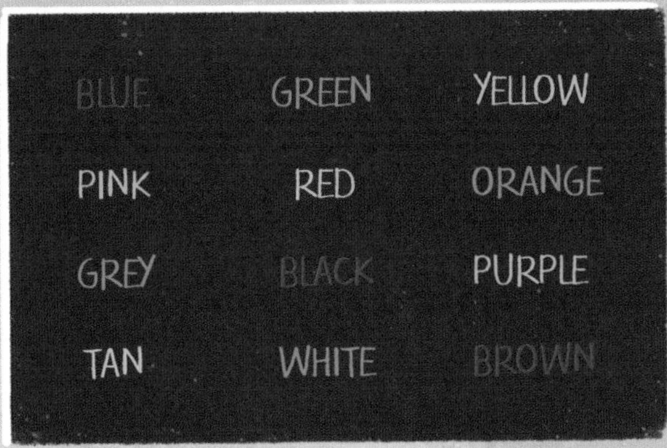

BLUE	GREEN	YELLOW
PINK	RED	ORANGE
GREY	BLACK	PURPLE
TAN	WHITE	BROWN

ame the colours of the words rather than reading the words. So, if ne word 'BLUE' is printed in a red colour, say 'RED'. Say the colours s fast as you can from left to right. It's not as easy as it looks!

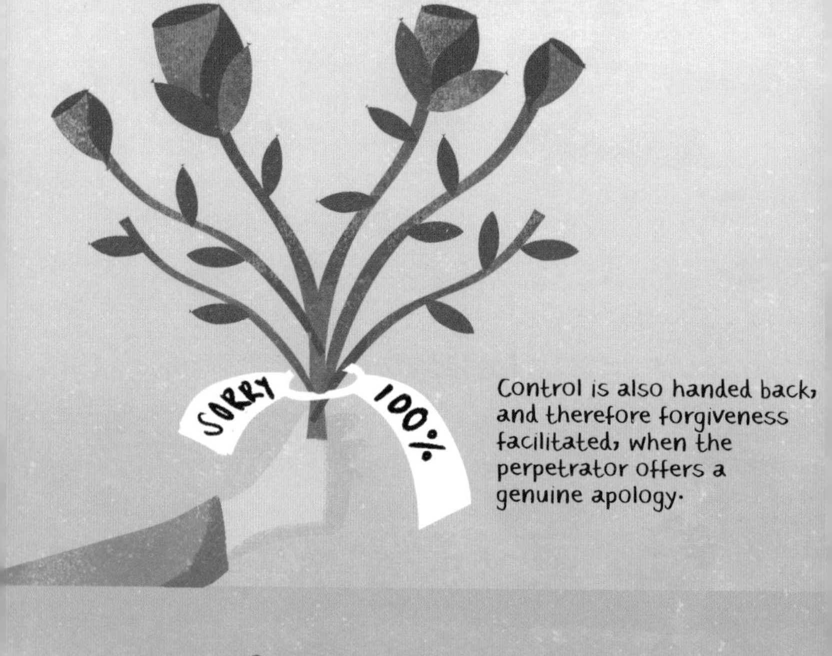
SORRY
100%

Control is also handed back, and therefore forgiveness facilitated, when the perpetrator offers a genuine apology.

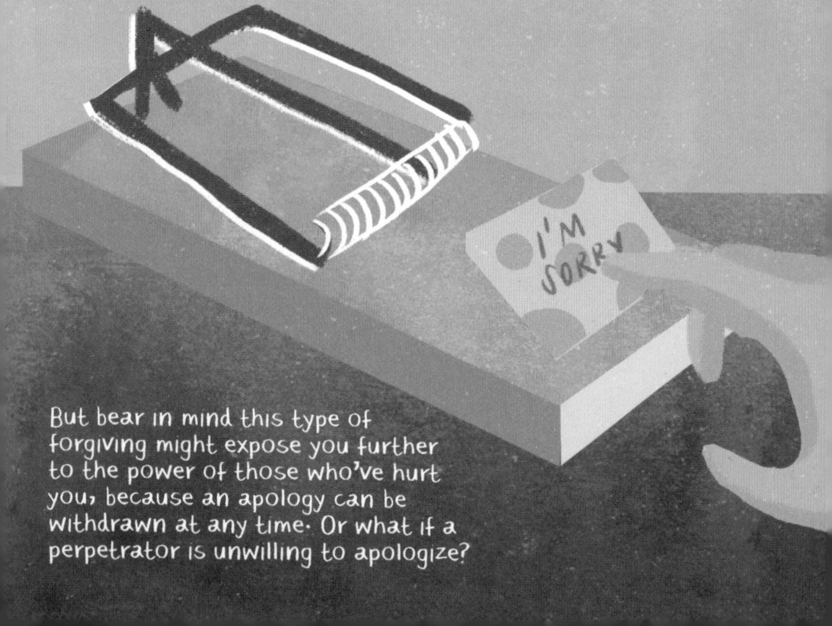
I'M SORRY

But bear in mind this type of forgiving might expose you further to the power of those who've hurt you, because an apology can be withdrawn at any time. Or what if a perpetrator is unwilling to apologize?

u don't need an apology in order to forgive.

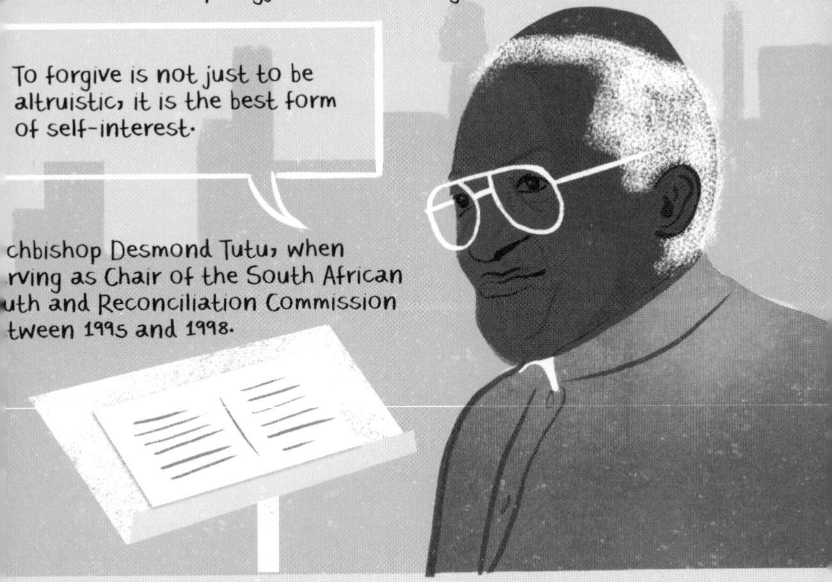
To forgive is not just to be altruistic, it is the best form of self-interest.

chbishop Desmond Tutu, when
rving as Chair of the South African
uth and Reconciliation Commission
tween 1995 and 1998.

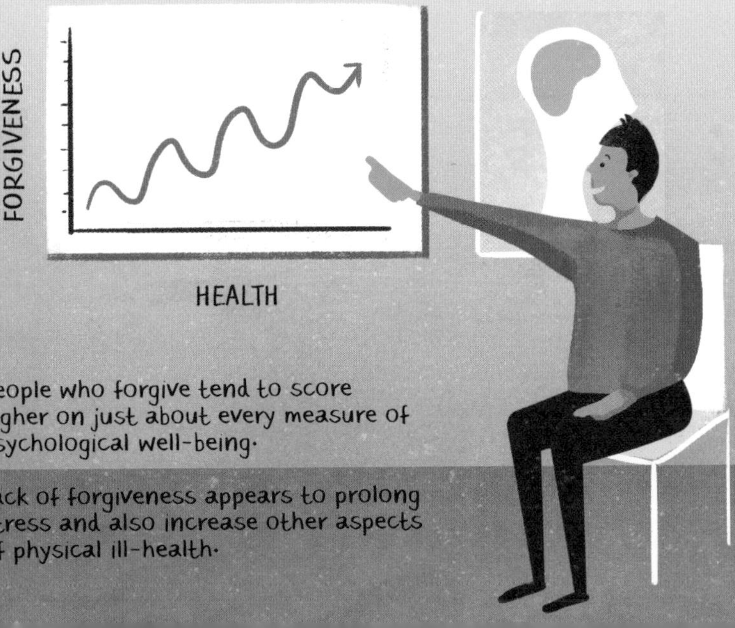
FORGIVENESS
HEALTH

People who forgive tend to score higher on just about every measure of psychological well-being.

Lack of forgiveness appears to prolong stress and also increase other aspects of physical ill-health.

But most momentous of all, it seems that the more you forgive the longer you may live.

The 'Forgive to Live' study collected data twice, with a 3-year gap, from a nationally representative sample of Americans who were 66 years old and over. It revealed that not forgiving was linked to living shorter lives. This was true irrespective of other personal factors, such as religion, socio-demographics or health.

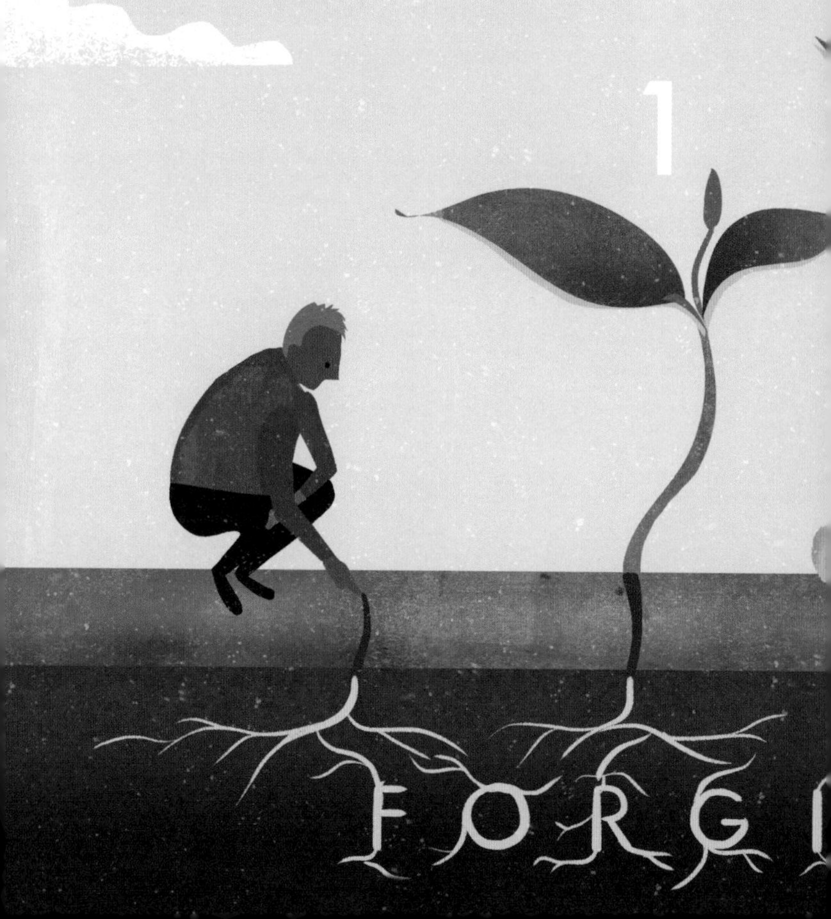

1
FORGI

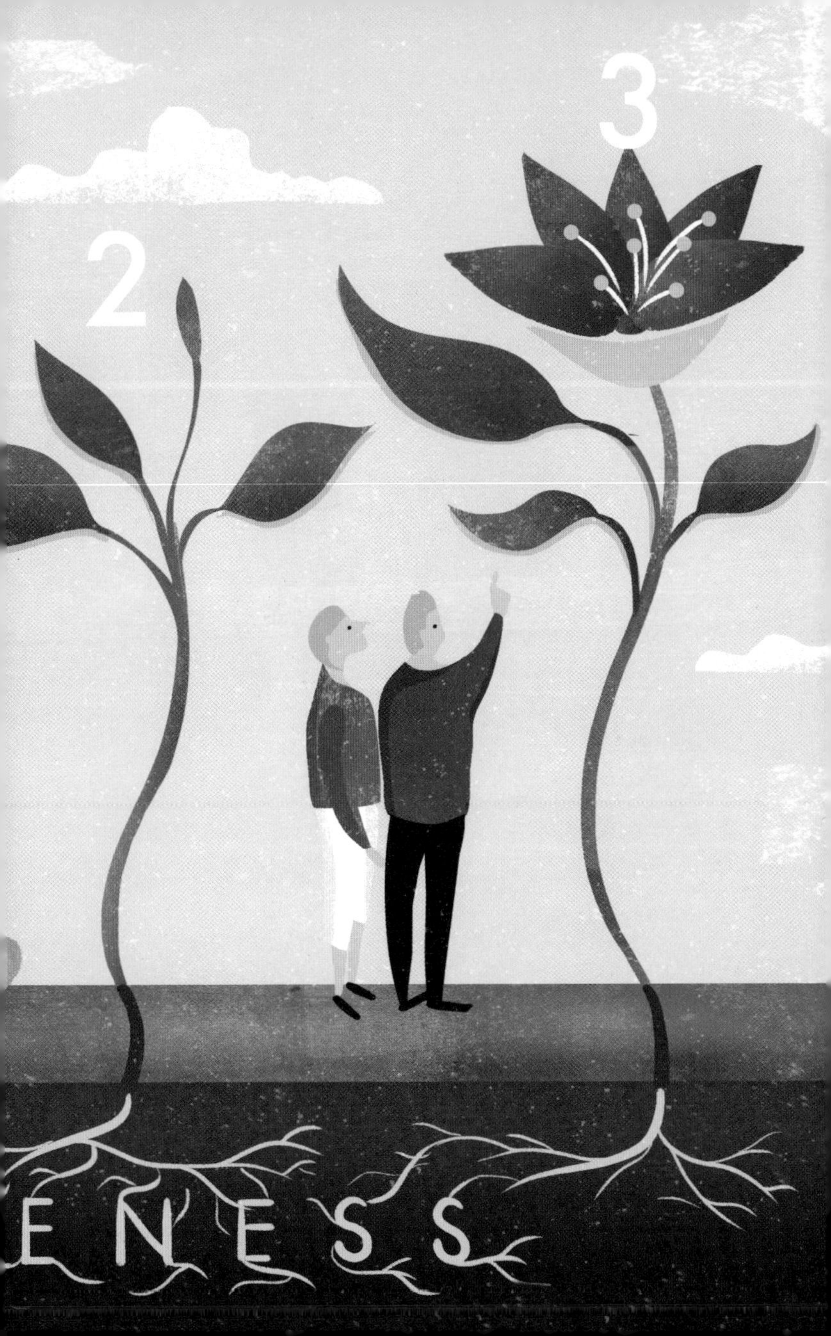
3
2
ENESS

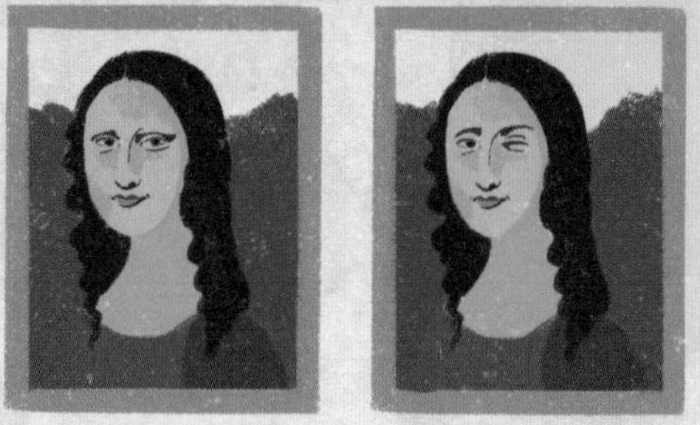

Despite the health benefits of forgiveness, it's important to distinguish forgiveness from what looks like forgiveness (pseudo-forgiveness), e.g. excusing or condoning bad behaviour.

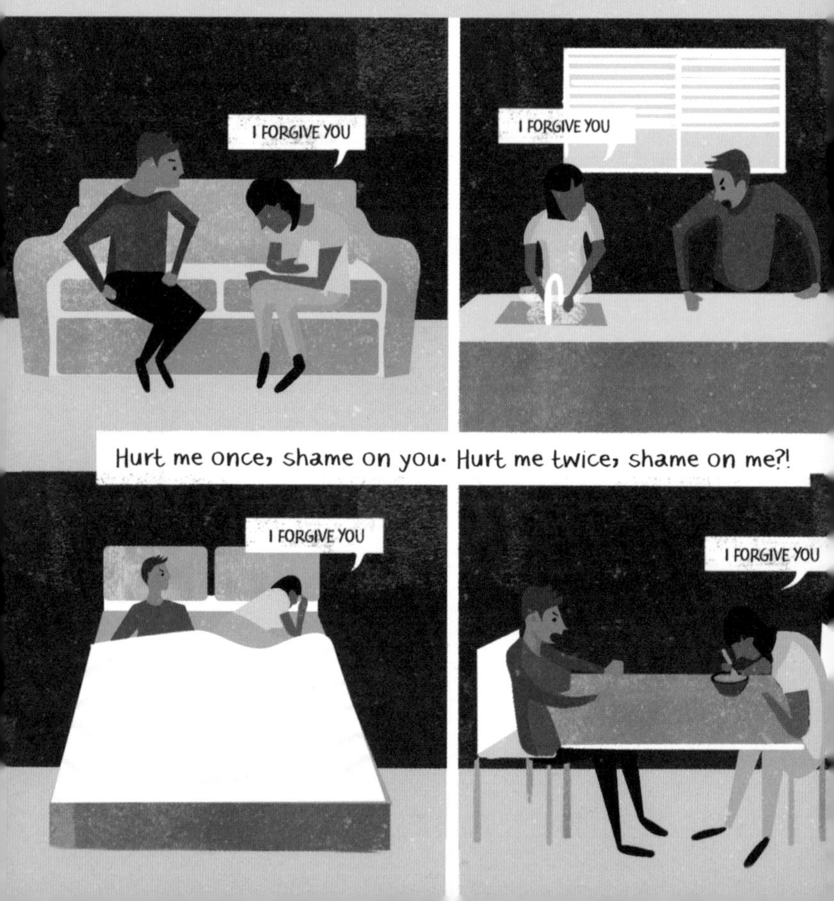
I FORGIVE YOU
I FORGIVE YOU
Hurt me once, shame on you. Hurt me twice, shame on me?!
I FORGIVE YOU
I FORGIVE YOU

That's folklore, but psychological research says that...

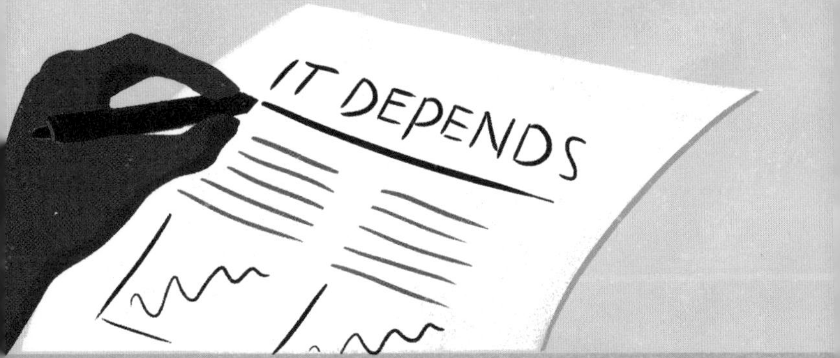
IT DEPENDS

Being forgiven can produce remorse and cooperation in the perpetrator.

Forgiveness may spread a culture of non-violence.

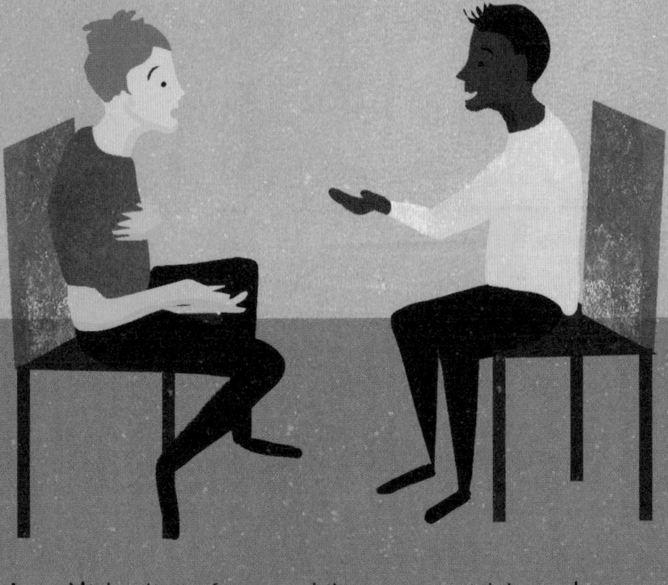

Arno Michaelis, a former white supremacist turned peace activist, explains: 'It was the unconditional forgiveness I was given by people who I once claimed to hate that demonstrated for me the way from there to here.'

BUT forgiving your harmer can be costly if the circumstances that led to the harm don't change.

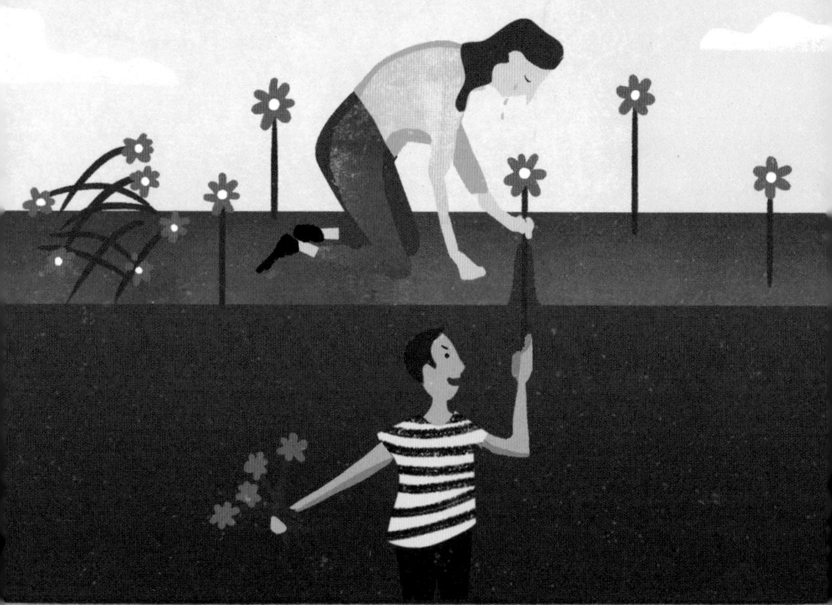

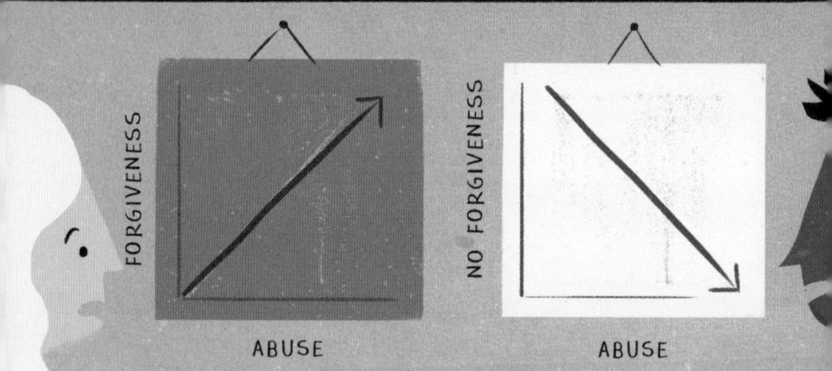
FORGIVENESS
ABUSE
NO FORGIVENESS
ABUSE

For example, researchers studied newlyweds during the first four years of their marriage. Of the people who reported incidents of psychological and physical violence by their partners, those who forgave their partners found the level of abuse remained the same, while those who were less forgiving found the level of abuse declined.

Remarkably, victims of physical abuse may 'forgive' their abusive partners because they feel ashamed and feel responsible for the abuse. But is it still forgiveness if forgiveness changes nothing about the abusive situation and leads to continued humiliation and dependency?

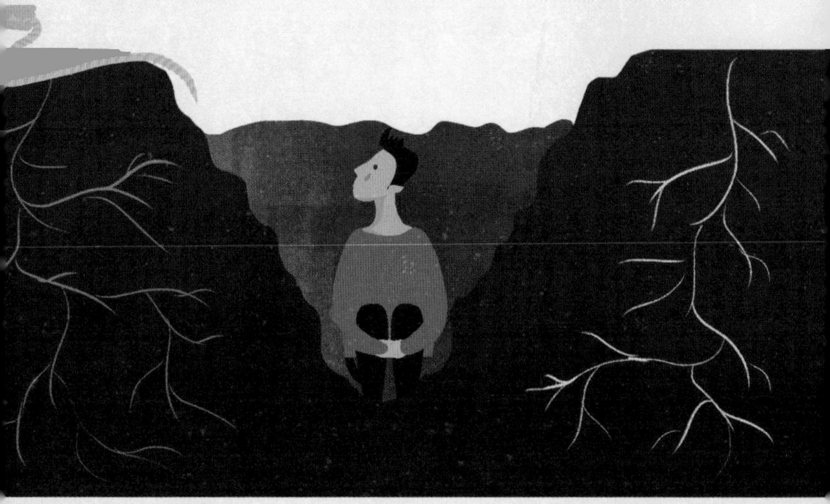

This dark side of forgiveness also holds true for large-scale historical grievances (e.g. grievances experienced by aboriginal people). This type of forgiveness (pseudo-forgiveness) confuses forgiving with condoning; it invites inaction and accepts the status quo.

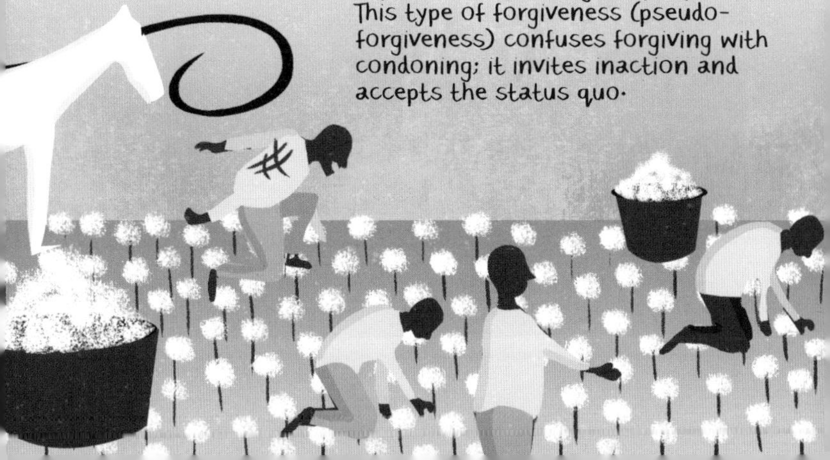

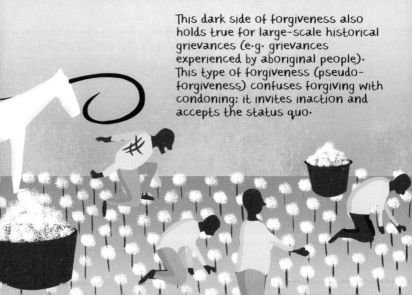

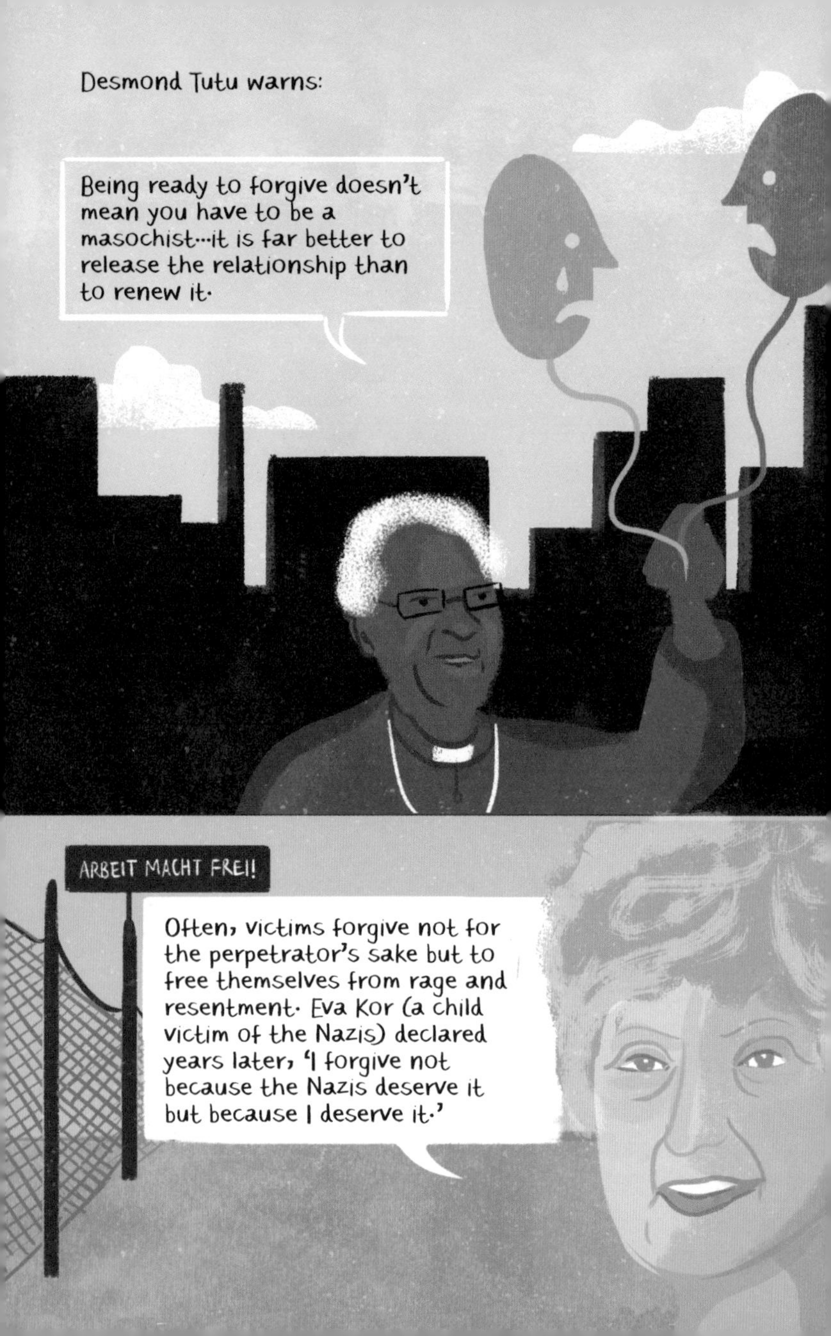
Desmond Tutu warns:
Being ready to forgive doesn't mean you have to be a masochist…it is far better to release the relationship than to renew it.
ARBEIT MACHT FREI!
Often, victims forgive not for the perpetrator's sake but to free themselves from rage and resentment. Eva Kor (a child victim of the Nazis) declared years later, 'I forgive not because the Nazis deserve it but because I deserve it.'

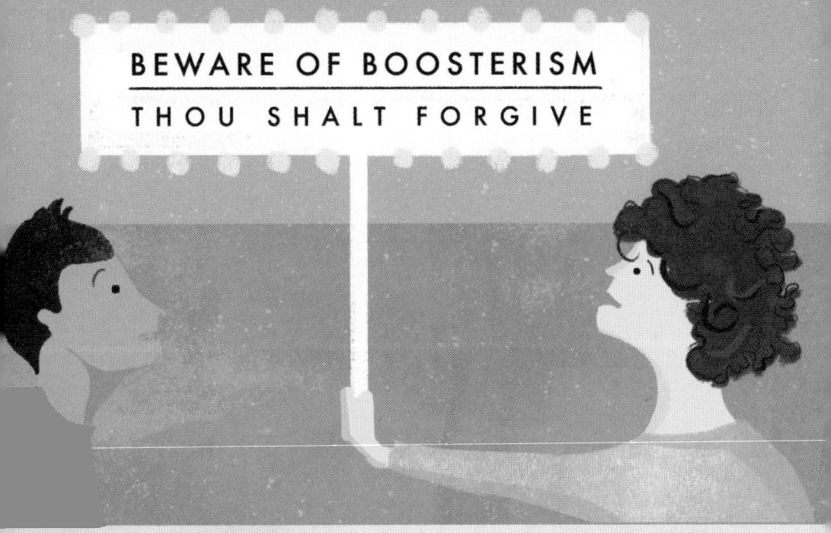
BEWARE OF BOOSTERISM
THOU SHALT FORGIVE

Forgiveness ceases to be helpful when it's offered as a universal prescription. Or if it's pushed or praised in an overly inflated way.

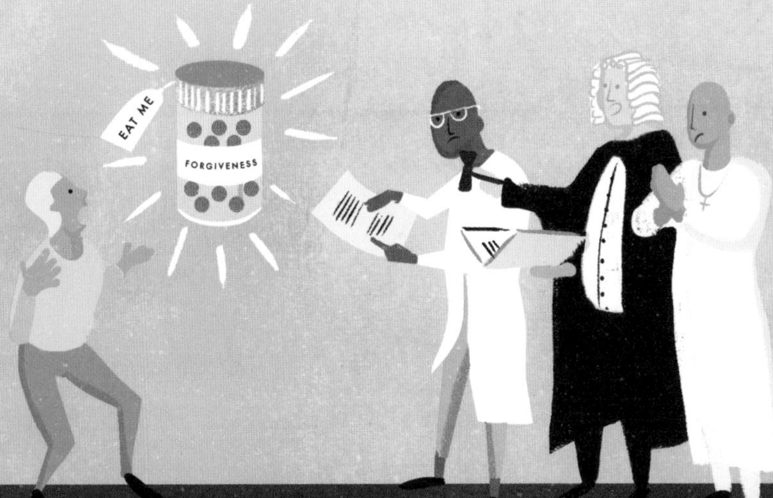
EAT ME
FORGIVENESS

'Forgiveness is a gift. It loses its power as gift if we make it a duty,' said restorative justice pioneer John Braithwaite.

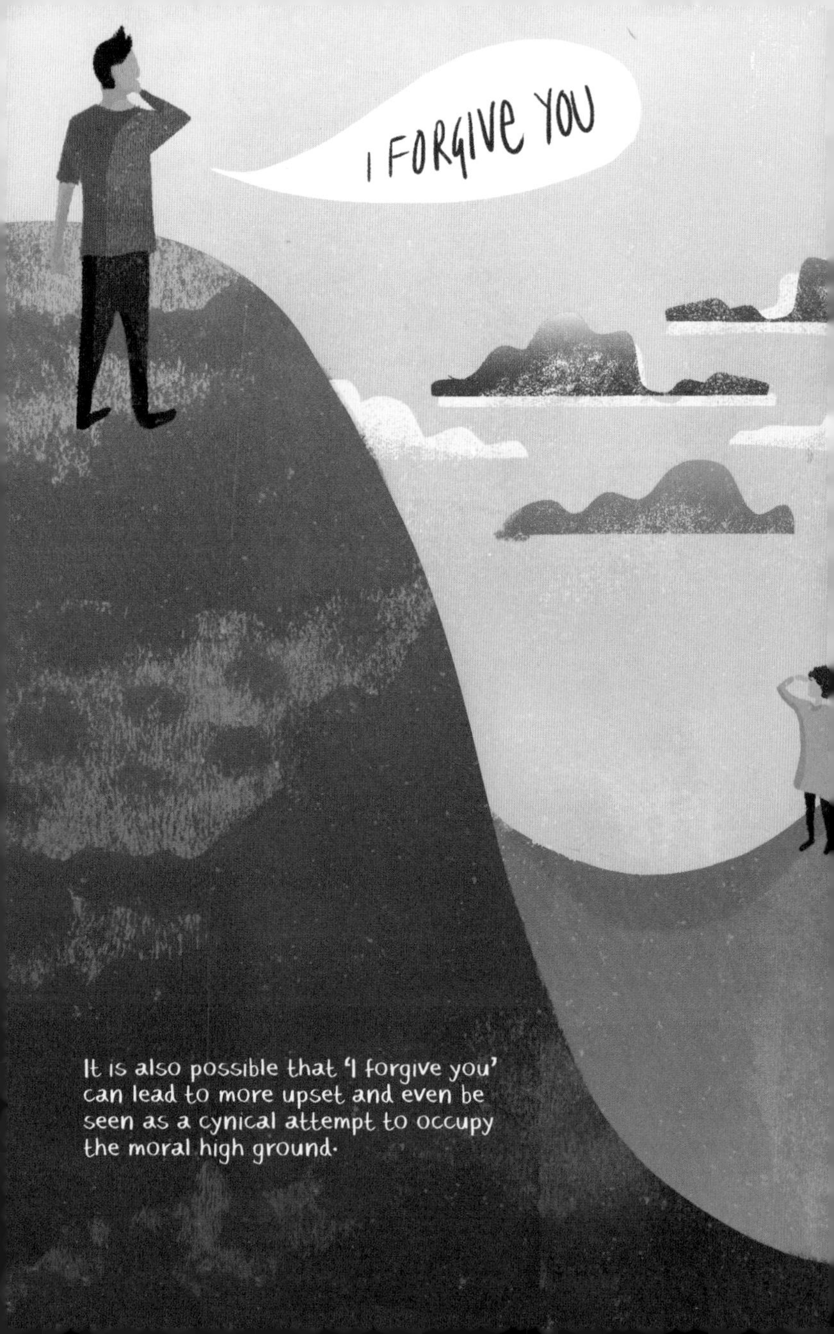
I FORGIVE YOU

It is also possible that 'I forgive you' can lead to more upset and even be seen as a cynical attempt to occupy the moral high ground.

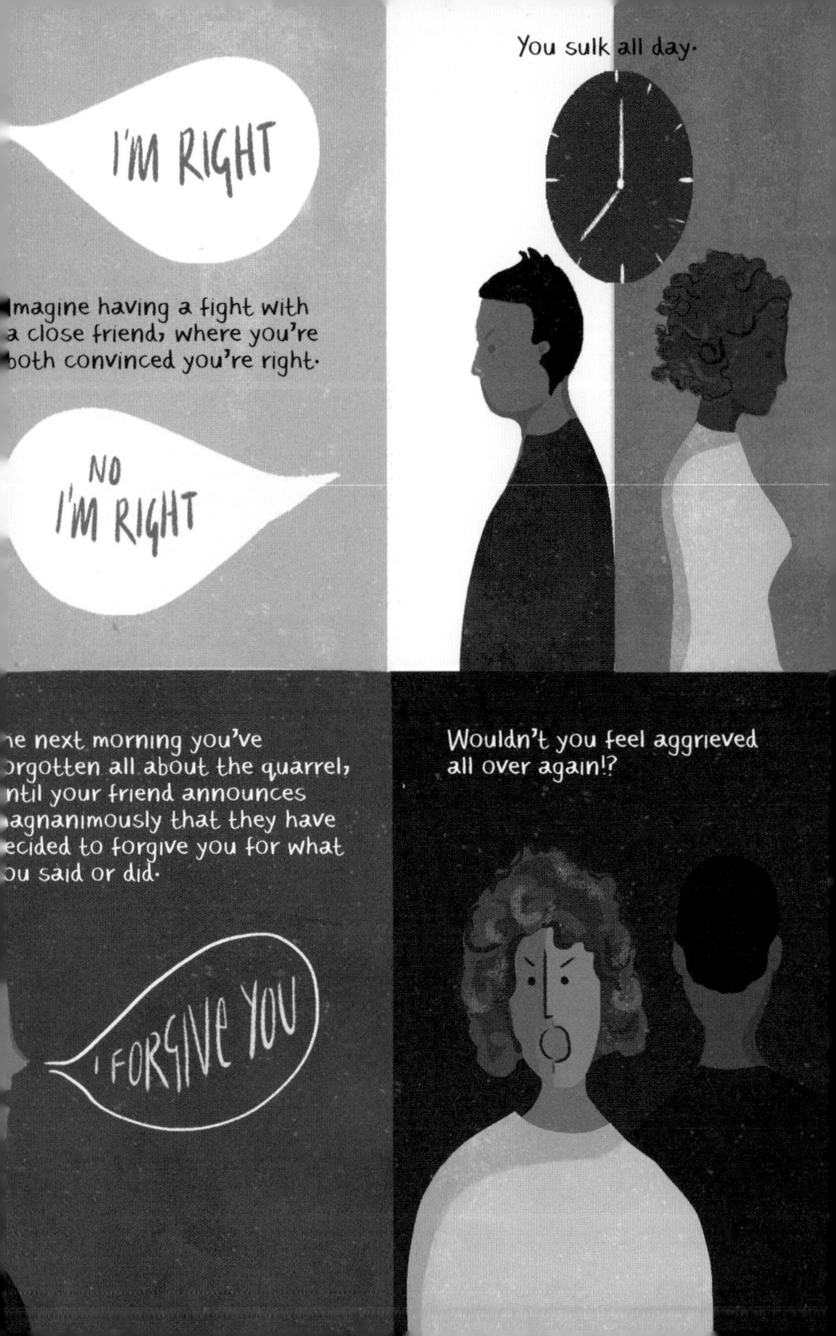
I'M RIGHT
Imagine having a fight with a close friend, where you're oth convinced you're right.
NO I'M RIGHT
You sulk all day.
e next morning you've orgotten all about the quarrel, ntil your friend announces agnanimously that they have ecided to forgive you for what ou said or did.
I FORGIVE YOU
Wouldn't you feel aggrieved all over again!?

Whether to forgive or not to forgive is entirely up to you. What might help you decide is to consider, what do I want from forgiveness?

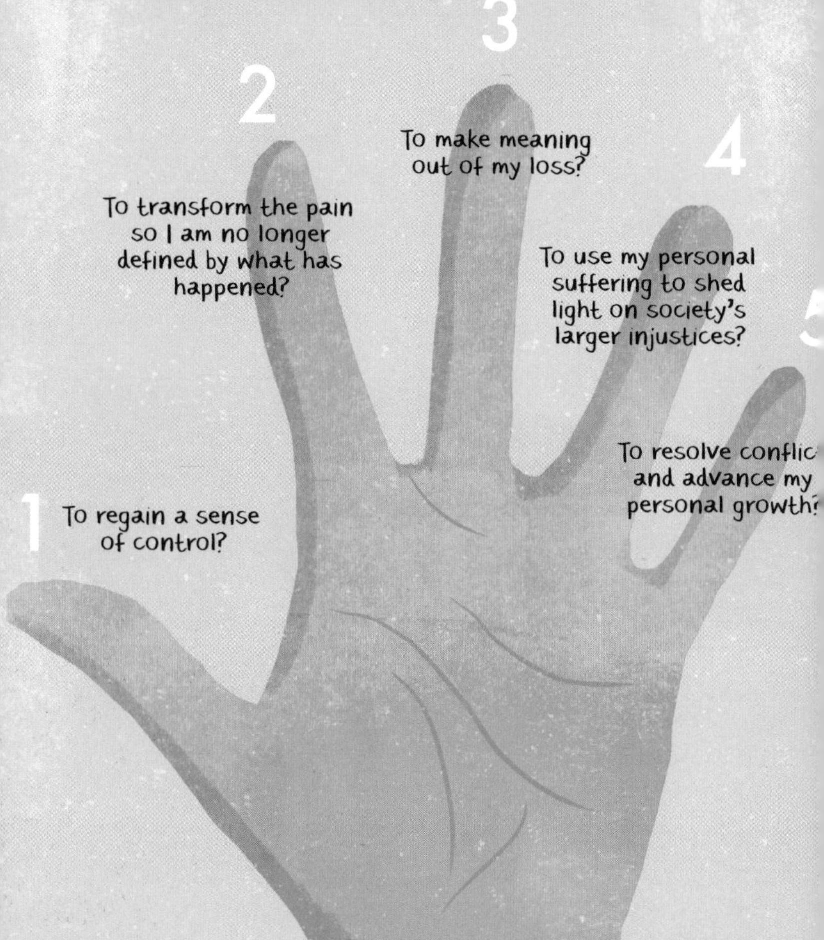
1
To regain a sense of control?
2
To transform the pain so I am no longer defined by what has happened?
3
To make meaning out of my loss?
4
To use my personal suffering to shed light on society's larger injustices?
To resolve conflic
and advance my personal growth?

Meandering through the complex landscape of forgiveness, it is clear that there are no short-cuts.

A great deal of learning comes from observing what others do.

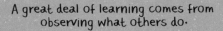

That's why the following skills or qualities are drawn from the real stories of victims (and perpetrators) who have transformed hurt and found resolution. In the next section we're going to open the Forgiveness Toolbox.

FORGIVENESS
WWW.THEFORGIVENESSTOOLBOX.CO
ACCEPTING RESPONSIBILITY
BUILDING BRIDGES
EMPATHY
BEYOND

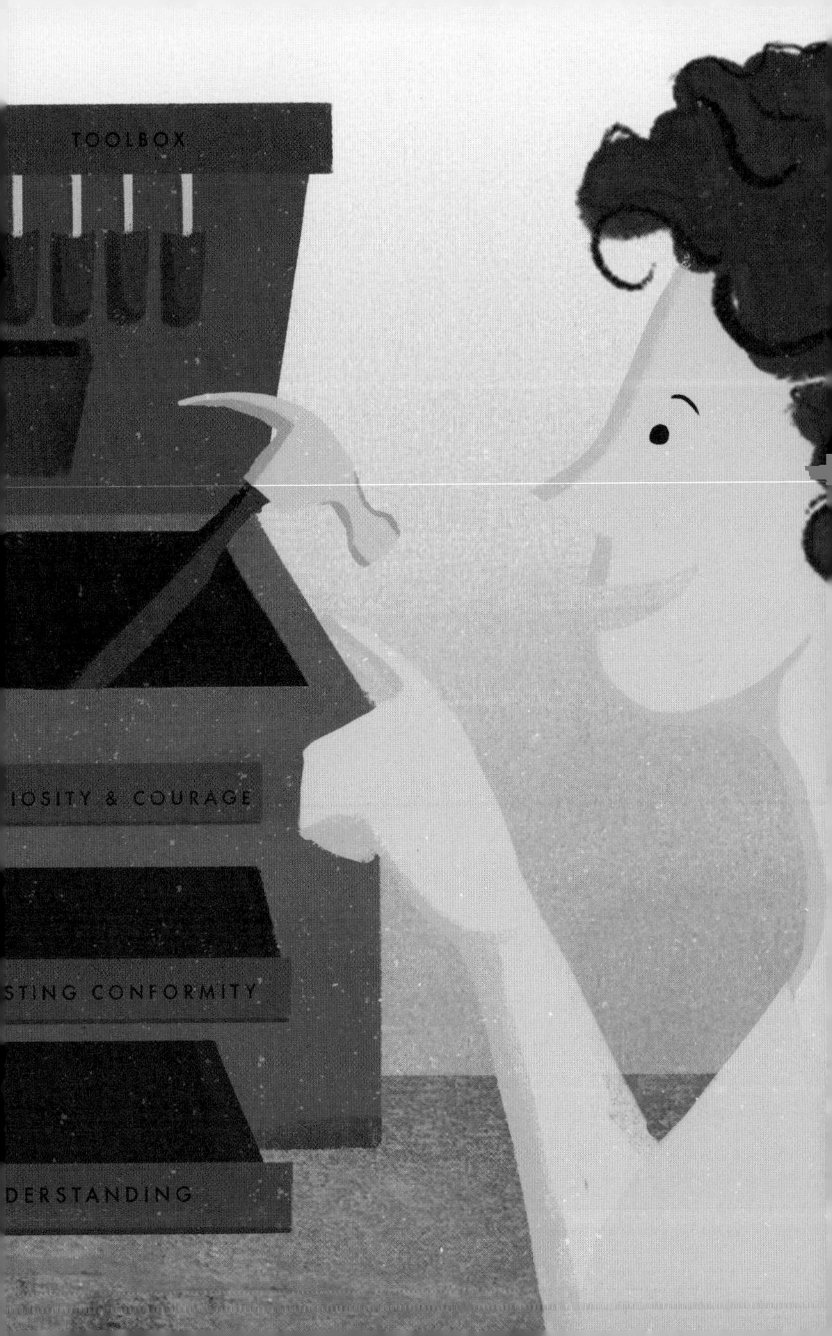
TOOLBOX
IOSITY & COURAGE
STING CONFORMITY
DERSTANDING

GO BEYOND 'WHY ME?'

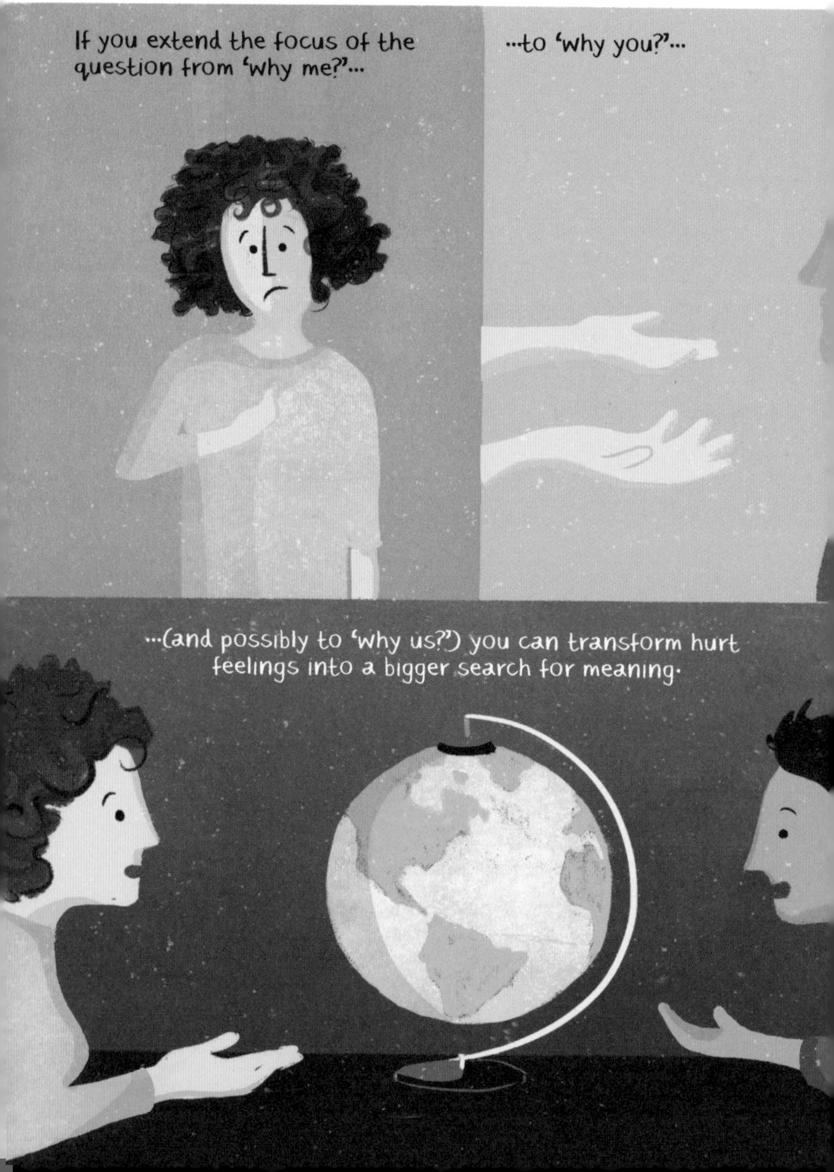
If you extend the focus of the question from 'why me?'...
...to 'why you?'...
...(and possibly to 'why us?') you can transform hurt feelings into a bigger search for meaning.

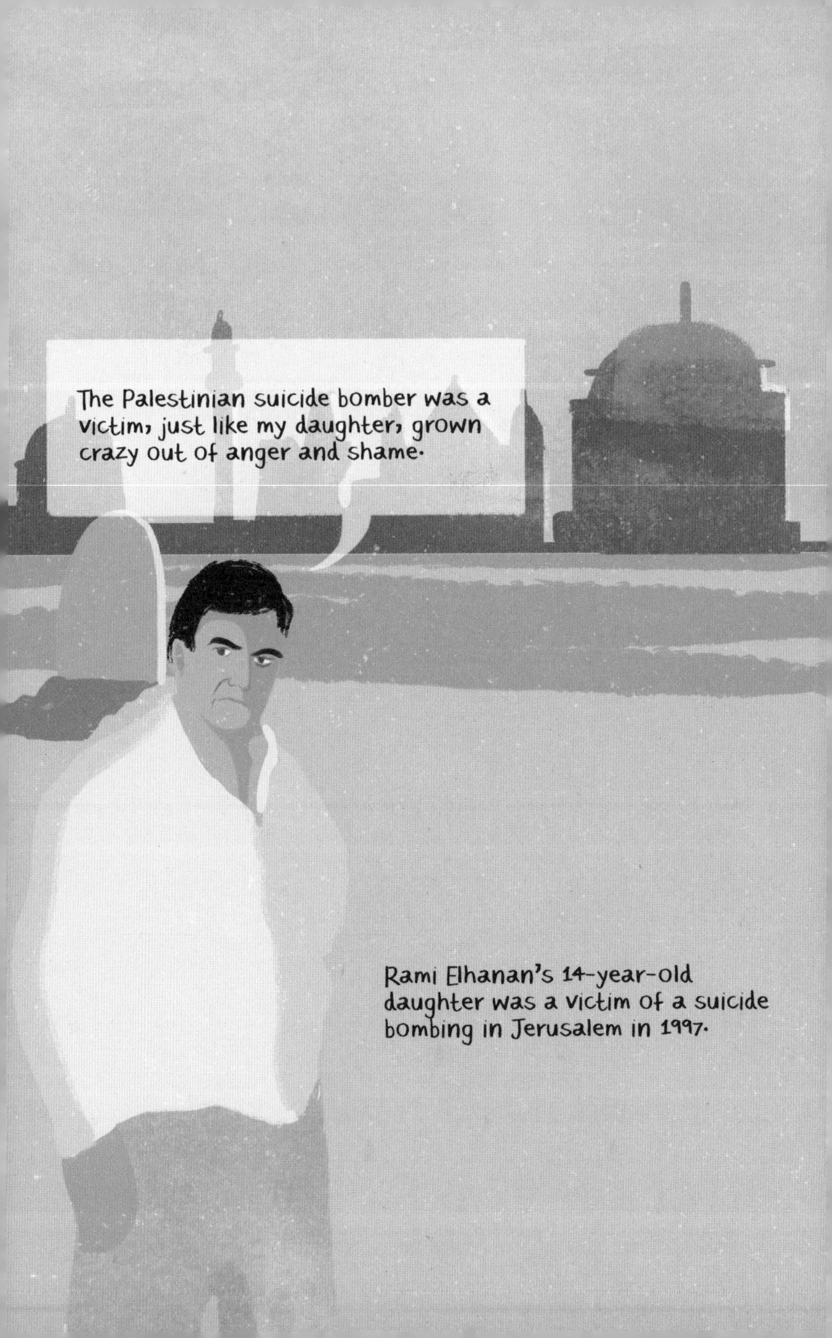
The Palestinian suicide bomber was a victim, just like my daughter, grown crazy out of anger and shame.
Rami Elhanan's 14-year-old daughter was a victim of a suicide bombing in Jerusalem in 1997.

BUILD BONDS OF SUFFERING

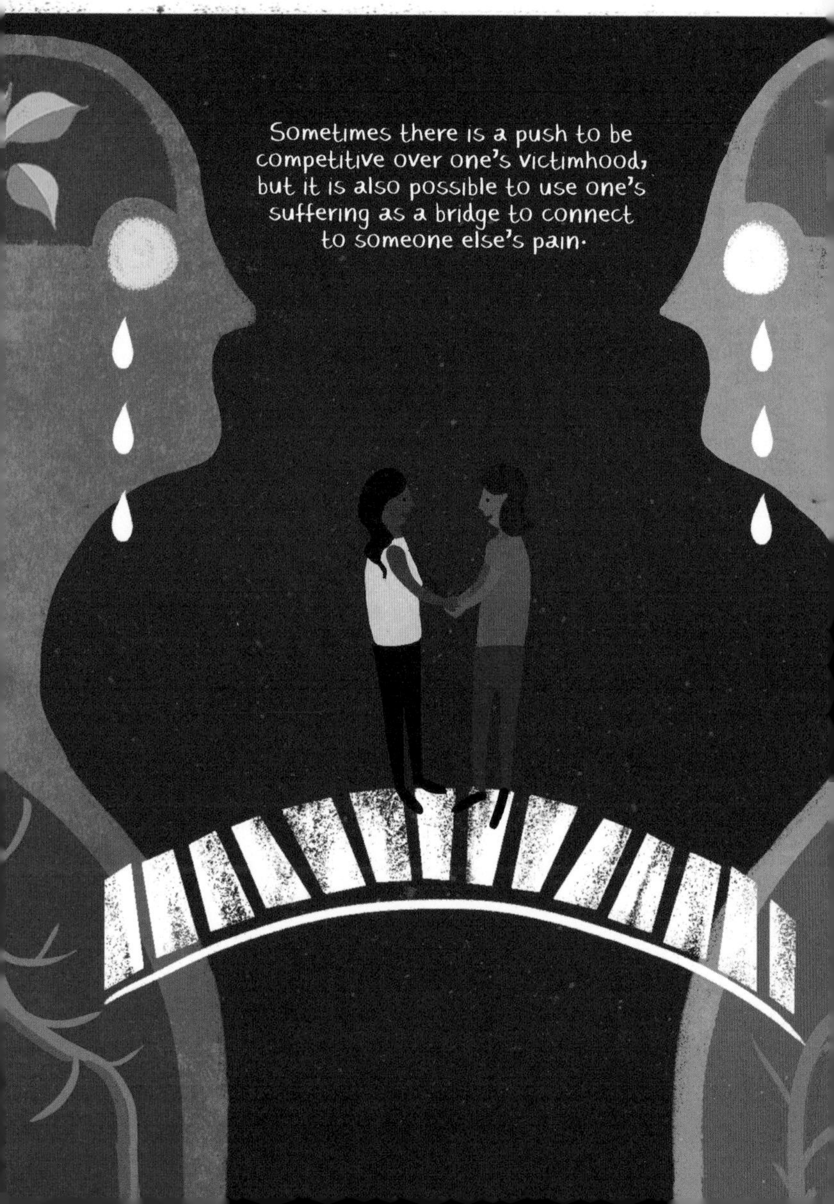
Sometimes there is a push to be competitive over one's victimhood, but it is also possible to use one's suffering as a bridge to connect to someone else's pain.

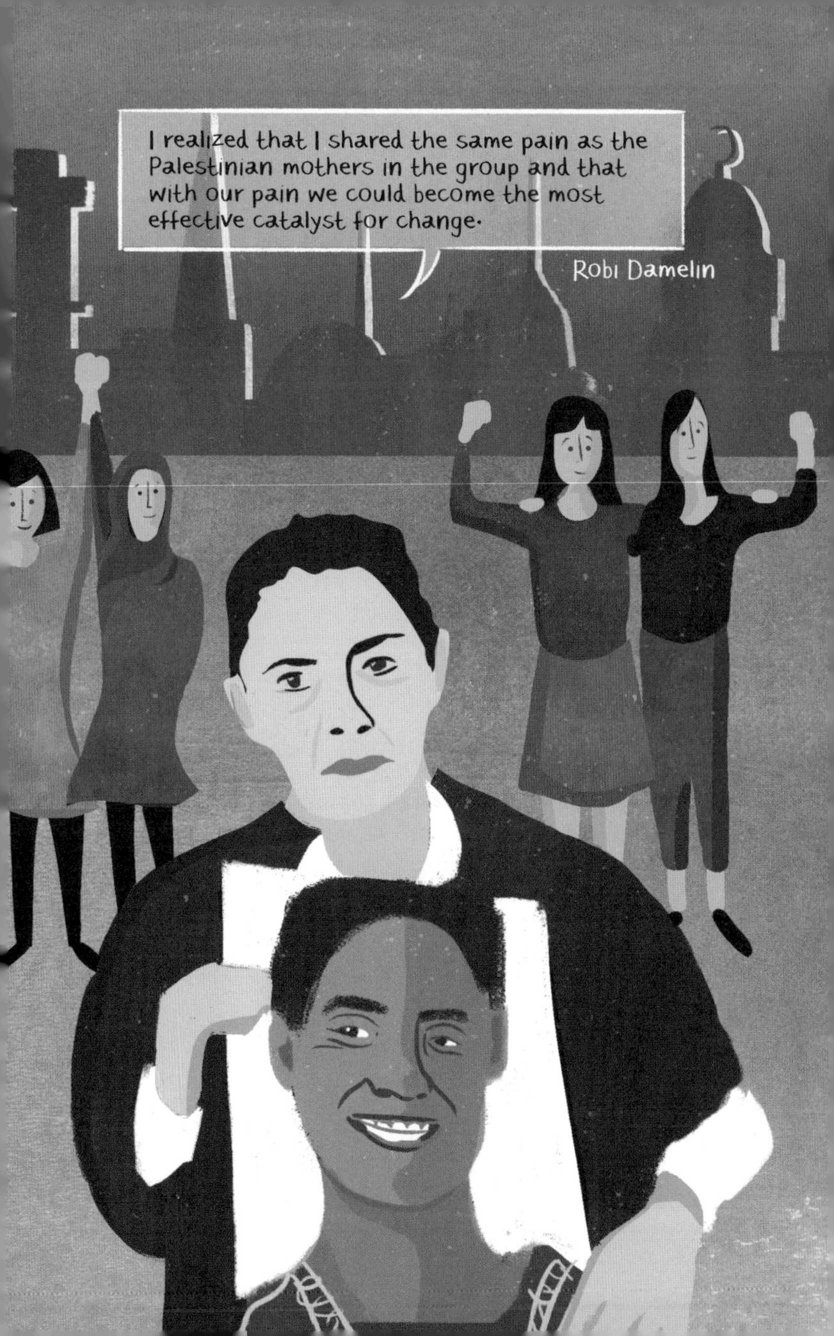
I realized that I shared the same pain as the Palestinian mothers in the group and that with our pain we could become the most effective catalyst for change.
Robi Damelin

TRY ON UNCOMFORTABLE NEW SHOES

It is hard to empathize with someone we don't like. Yet, practising this skill can bring insight into that person's feelings and actions and help us understand what motivated them to cause our suffering.

!!!
???

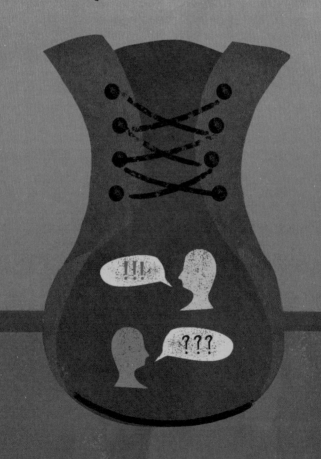

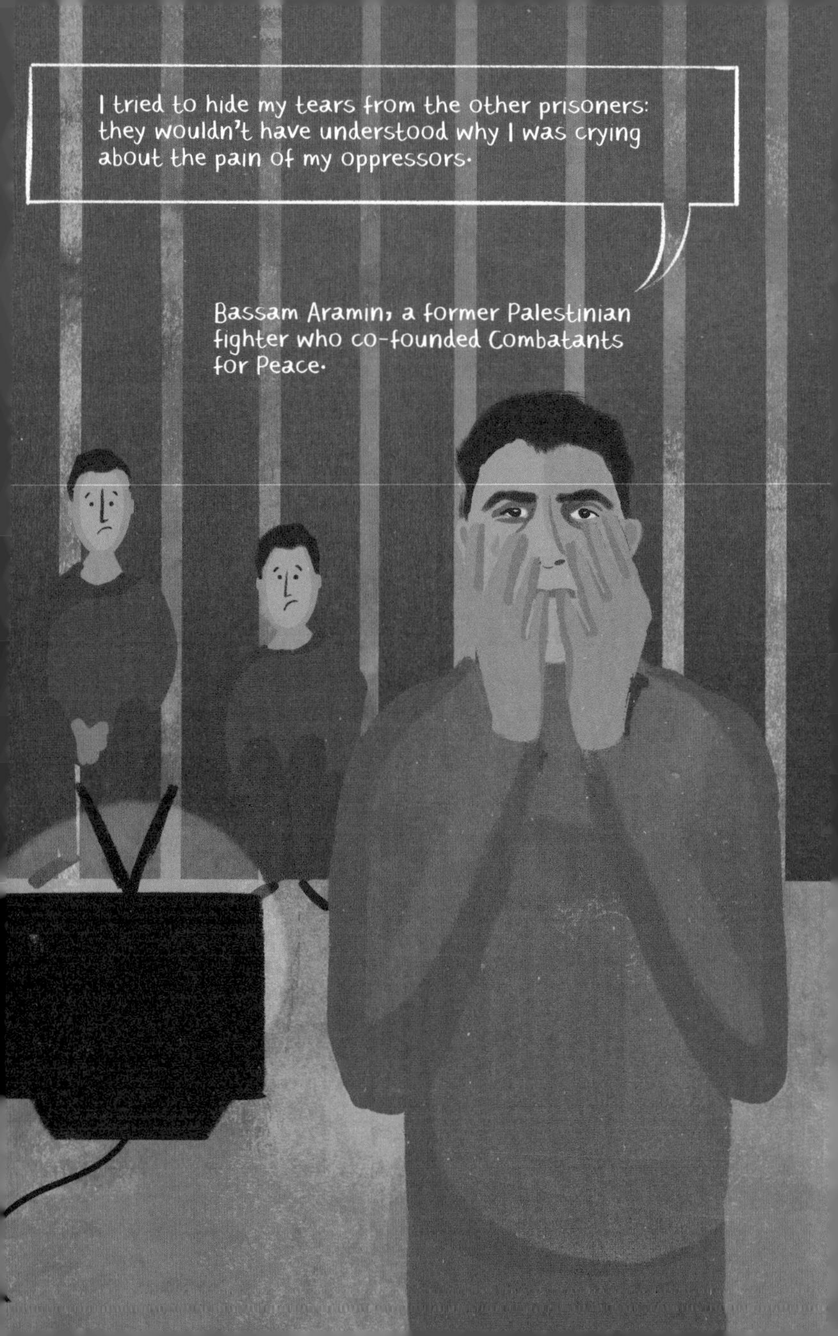
I tried to hide my tears from the other prisoners: they wouldn't have understood why I was crying about the pain of my oppressors.
Bassam Aramin, a former Palestinian fighter who co-founded Combatants for Peace.

BE CURIOUS

To assist you with the previous skills, you will need to develop curiosity. Curiosity opens up new worlds and possibilities. It invites you to imagine. Forgiving people tend to be broad, flexible thinkers.

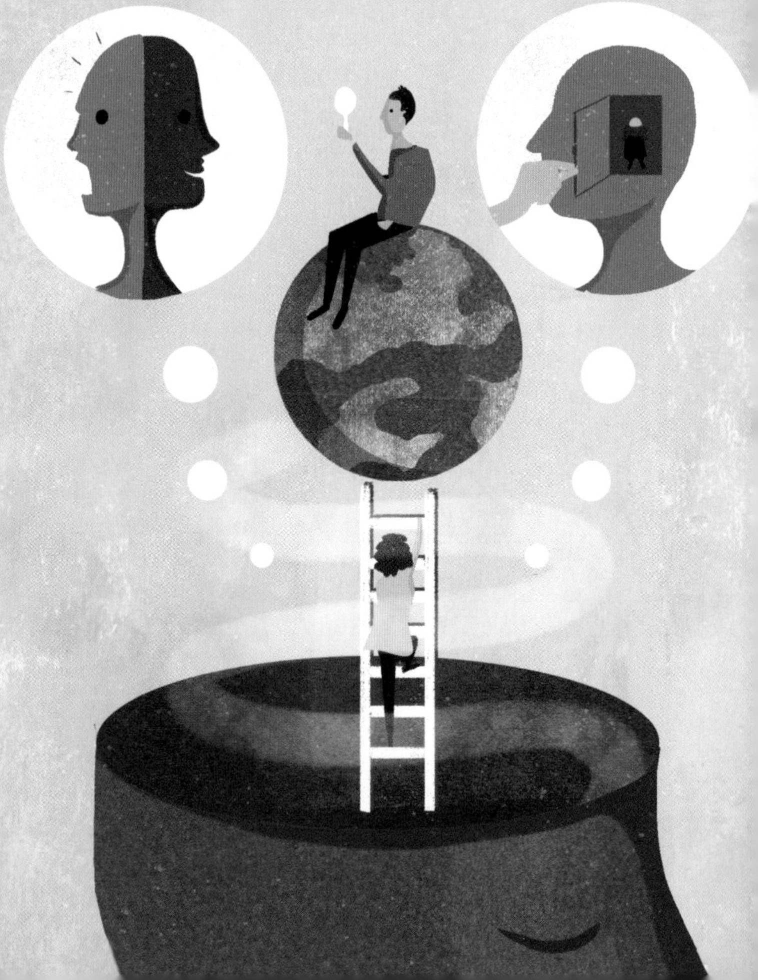

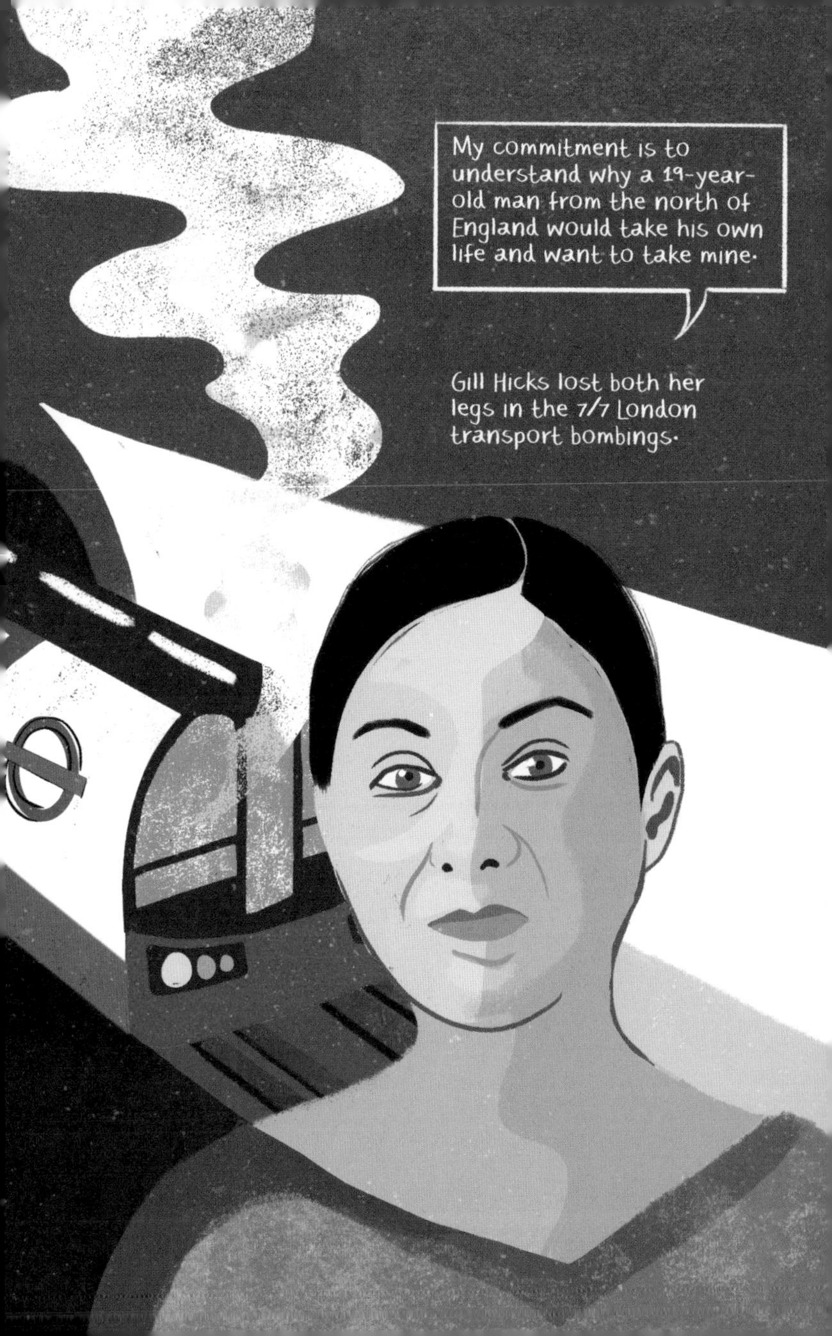
My commitment is to understand why a 19-year-old man from the north of England would take his own life and want to take mine.
Gill Hicks lost both her legs in the 7/7 London transport bombings.

BE COURAGEOUS

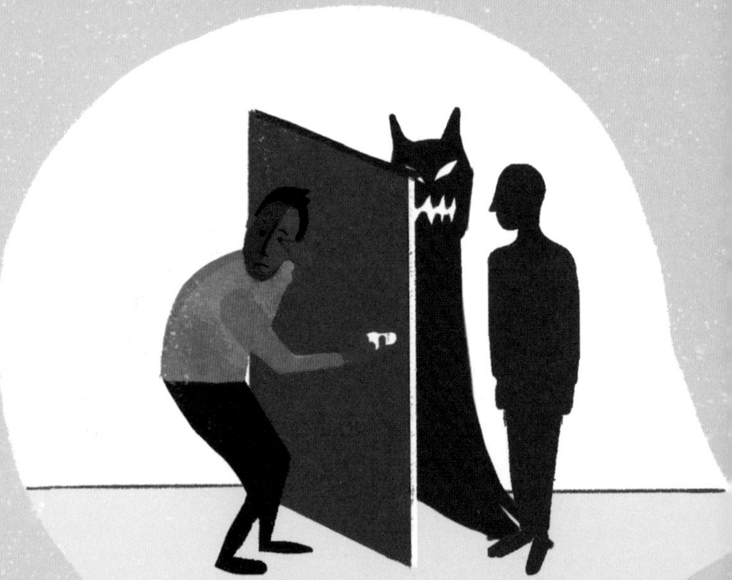

But often it's quite scary to come close to the perpetrator (even mentally), which is why it takes courage too.

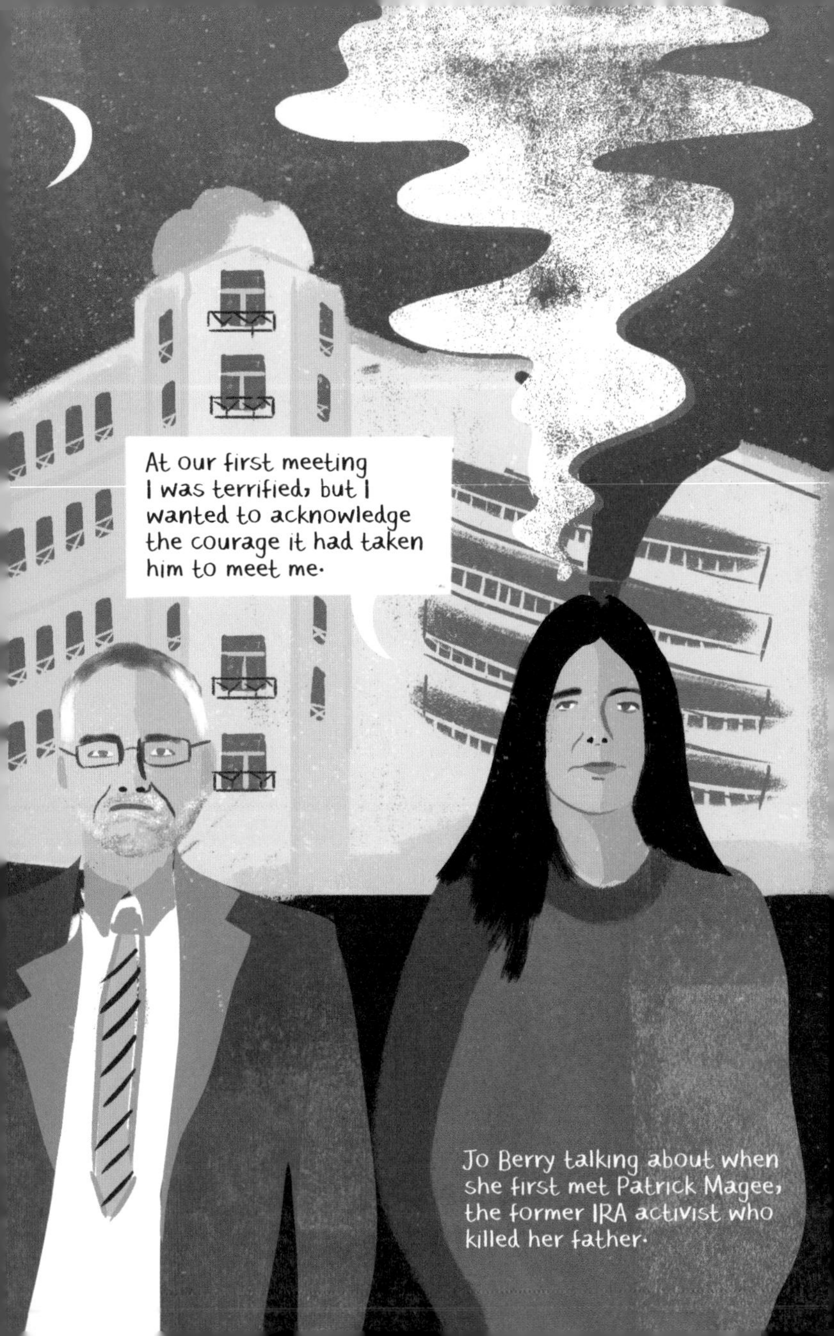
At our first meeting I was terrified, but I wanted to acknowledge the courage it had taken him to meet me.
Jo Berry talking about when she first met Patrick Magee, the former IRA activist who killed her father.

ACCEPT RESPONSIBILITY

As we've seen earlier, being harmed reduces our sense of self-control. But becoming aware of how each of us (as individuals and as part of a group) has contributed to a situation can actually be empowering.

In some cases, victims realize they too have been perpetrators:

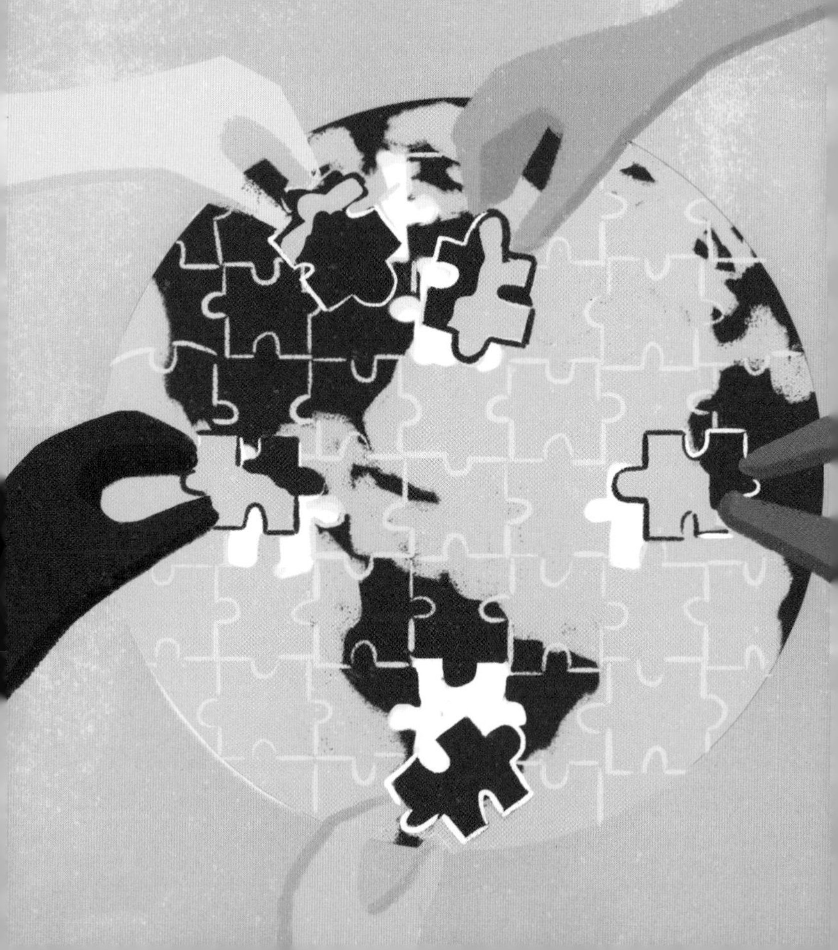

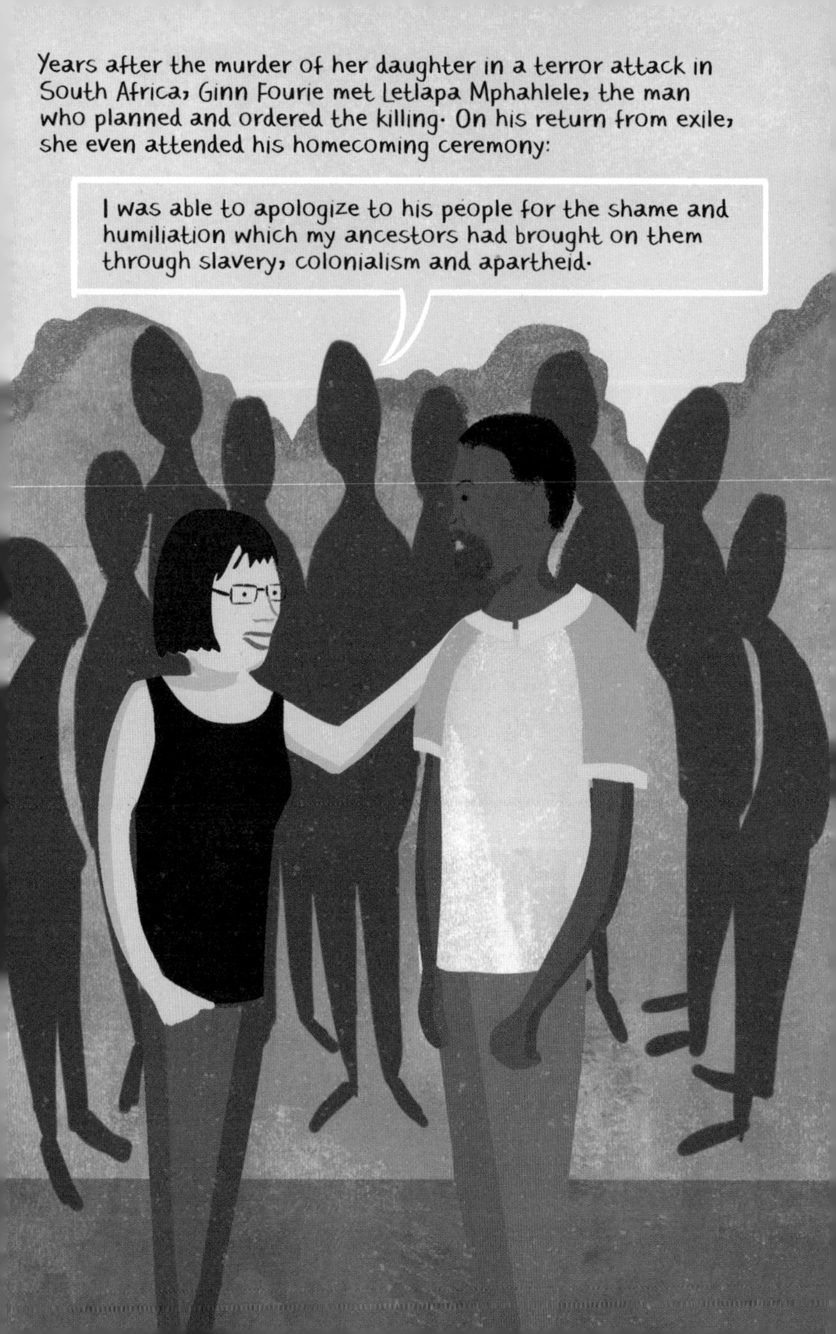
Years after the murder of her daughter in a terror attack in South Africa, Ginn Fourie met Letlapa Mphahlele, the man who planned and ordered the killing. On his return from exile, she even attended his homecoming ceremony:
I was able to apologize to his people for the shame and humiliation which my ancestors had brought on them through slavery, colonialism and apartheid.

RESIST CONFORMITY

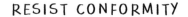

To forgive, you have to be prepared to be an outsider and to question the assumptions, norms and values of your society.

It takes some nerve to forgive because it can be a lonely place. Those around you may see it as an act of betrayal or feel angry and vengeful on your behalf.

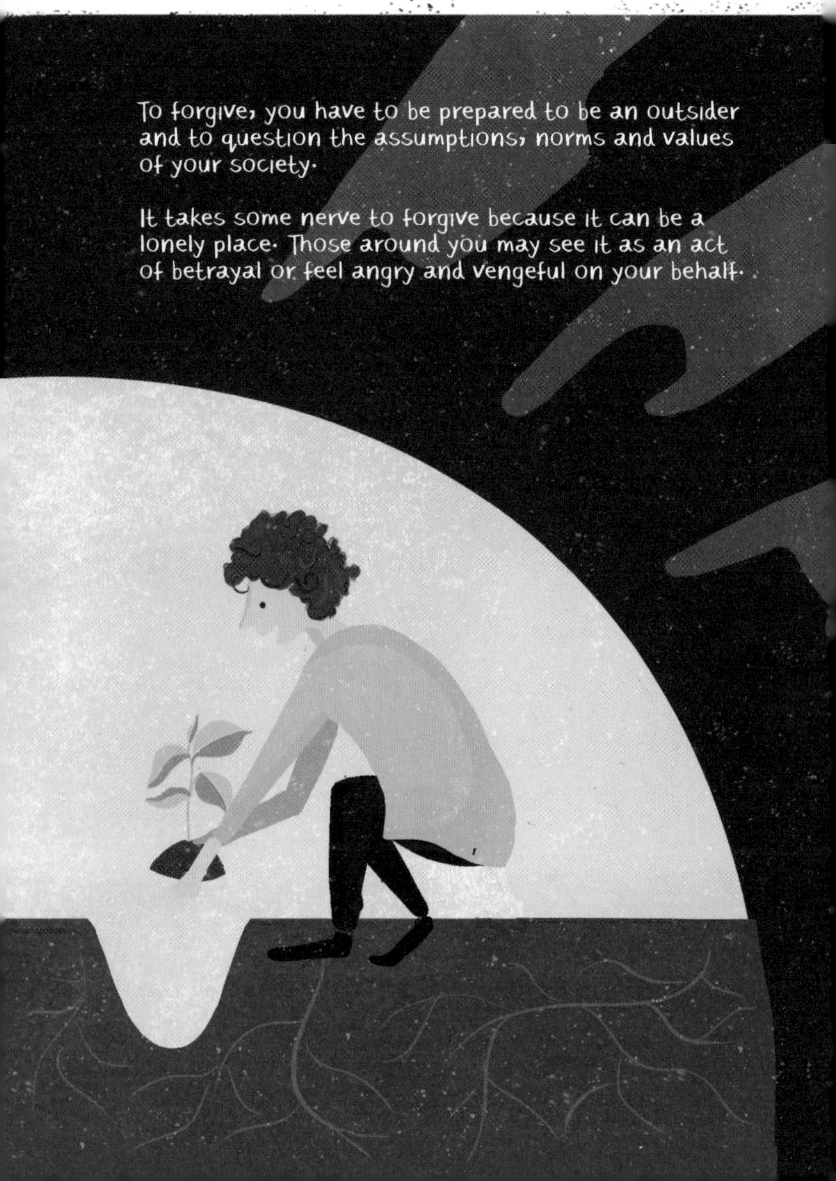

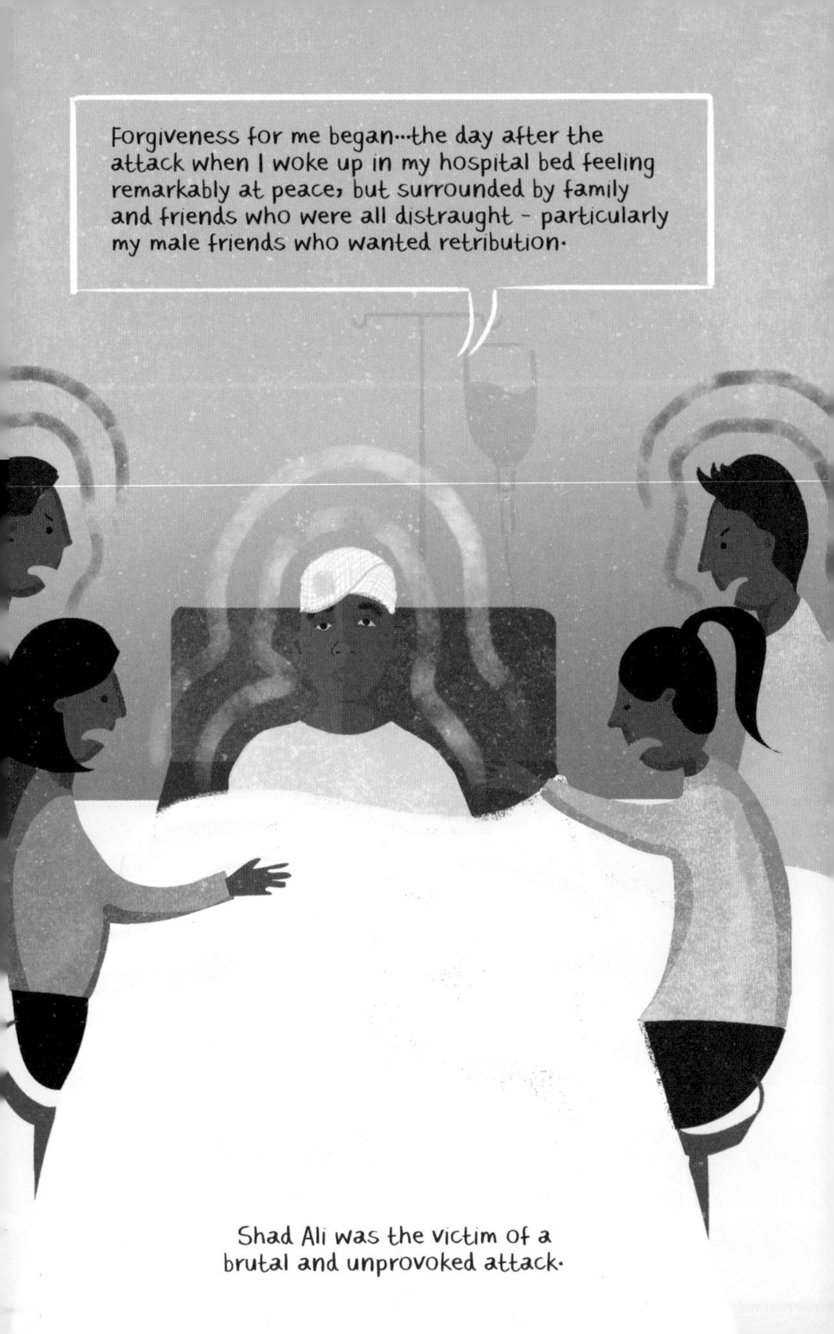
Forgiveness for me began...the day after the attack when I woke up in my hospital bed feeling remarkably at peace, but surrounded by family and friends who were all distraught - particularly my male friends who wanted retribution.
Shad Ali was the victim of a brutal and unprovoked attack.

LEAVE RESENTMENT BEHIND

All the above skills can help to release resentment. When we are no longer defined by those who have damaged us, when we are reminded that no one is born evil (including our enemies), then we can transform hate and find significance and even benefit in what has hurt us.

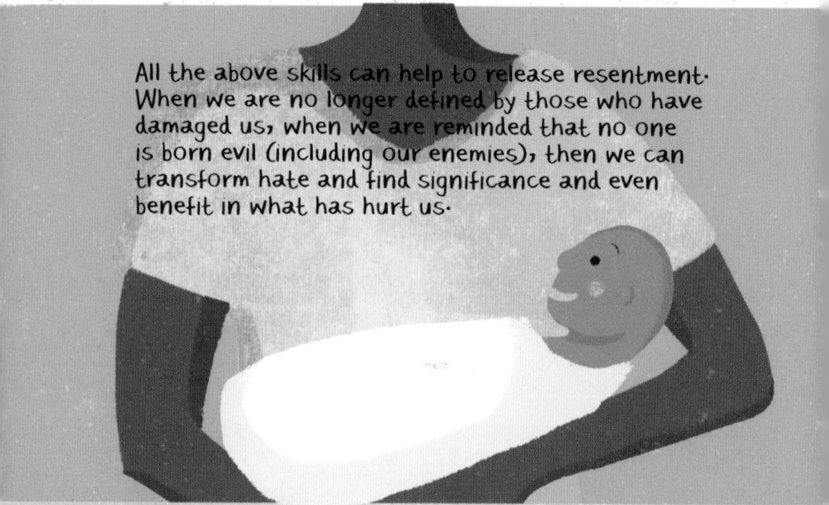

As Leonard Cohen said, 'There's a crack in everything, that's how the light gets in.'

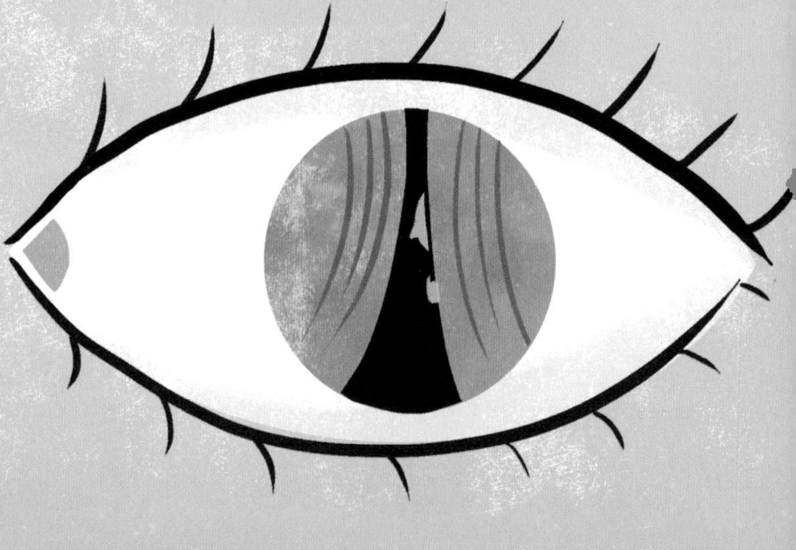

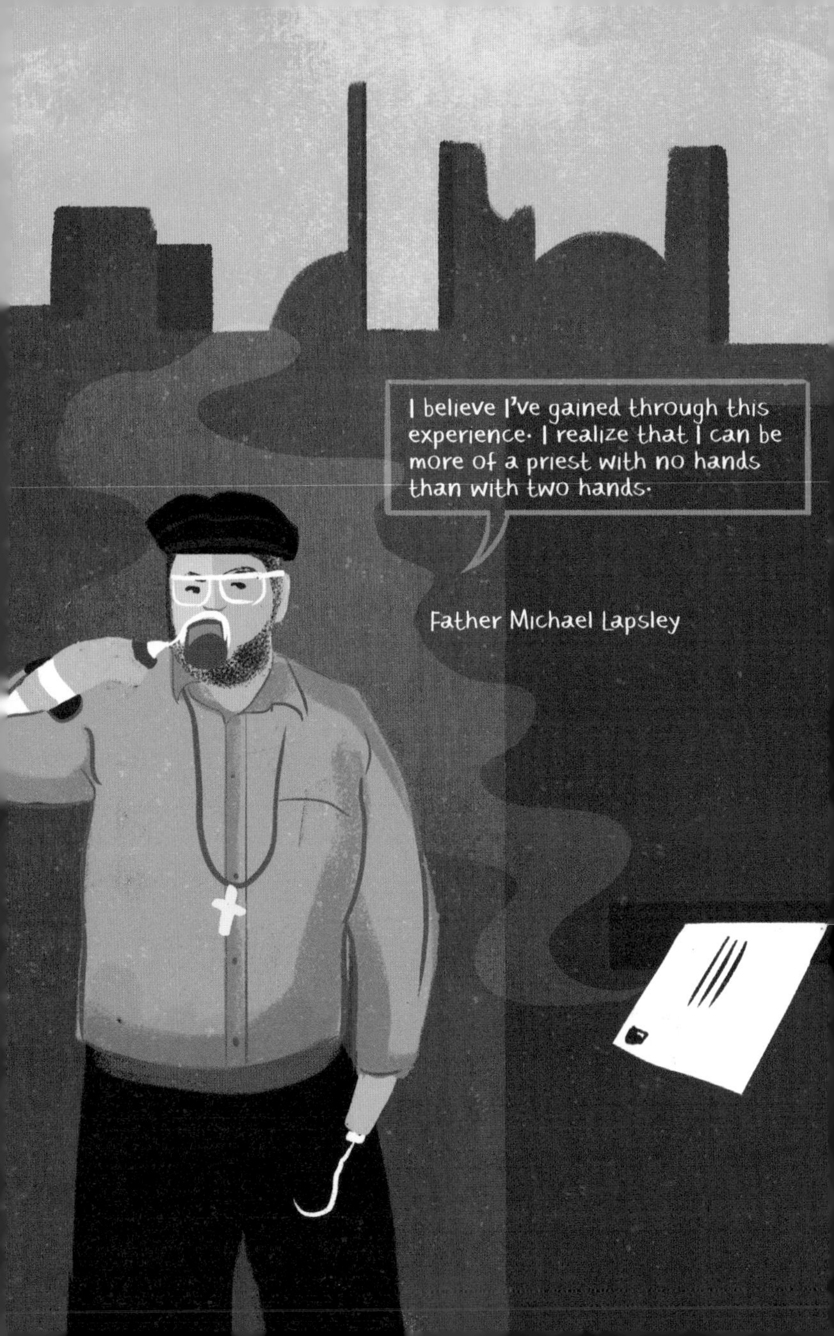
I believe I've gained through this experience. I realize that I can be more of a priest with no hands than with two hands.
Father Michael Lapsley

It's probably obvious by now that the more you examine forgiveness, the more complex and curious the topic becomes.

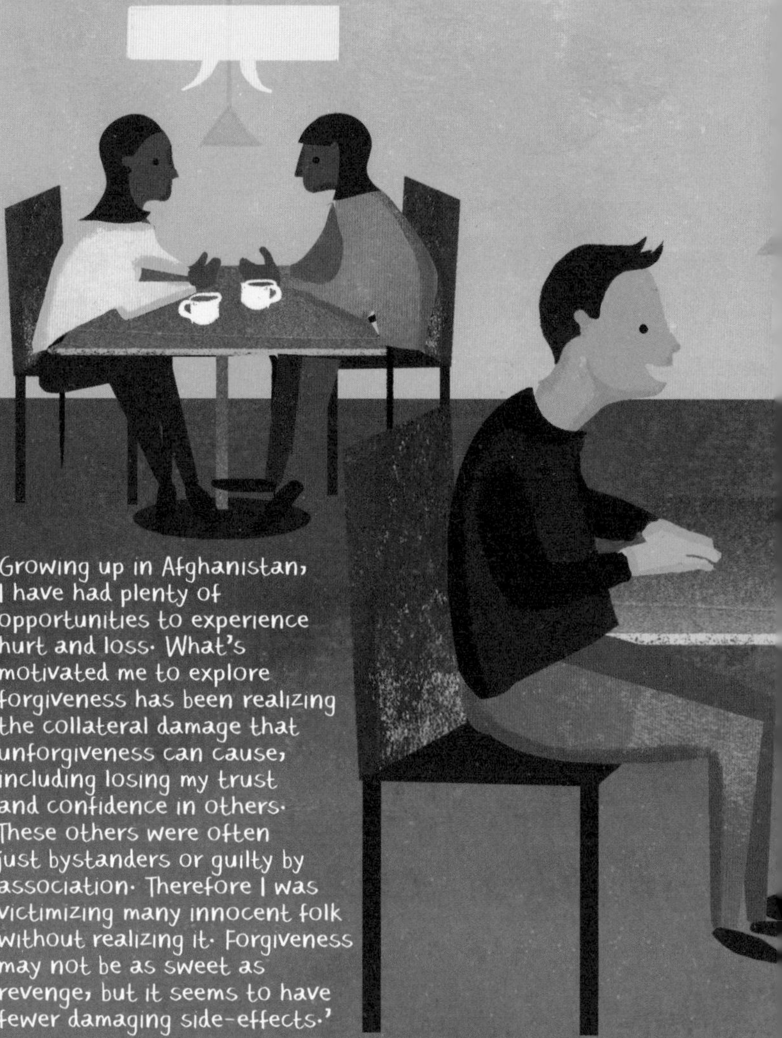

'Growing up in Afghanistan, I have had plenty of opportunities to experience hurt and loss. What's motivated me to explore forgiveness has been realizing the collateral damage that unforgiveness can cause, including losing my trust and confidence in others. These others were often just bystanders or guilty by association. Therefore I was victimizing many innocent folk without realizing it. Forgiveness may not be as sweet as revenge, but it seems to have fewer damaging side-effects.'

DR MASI NOOR

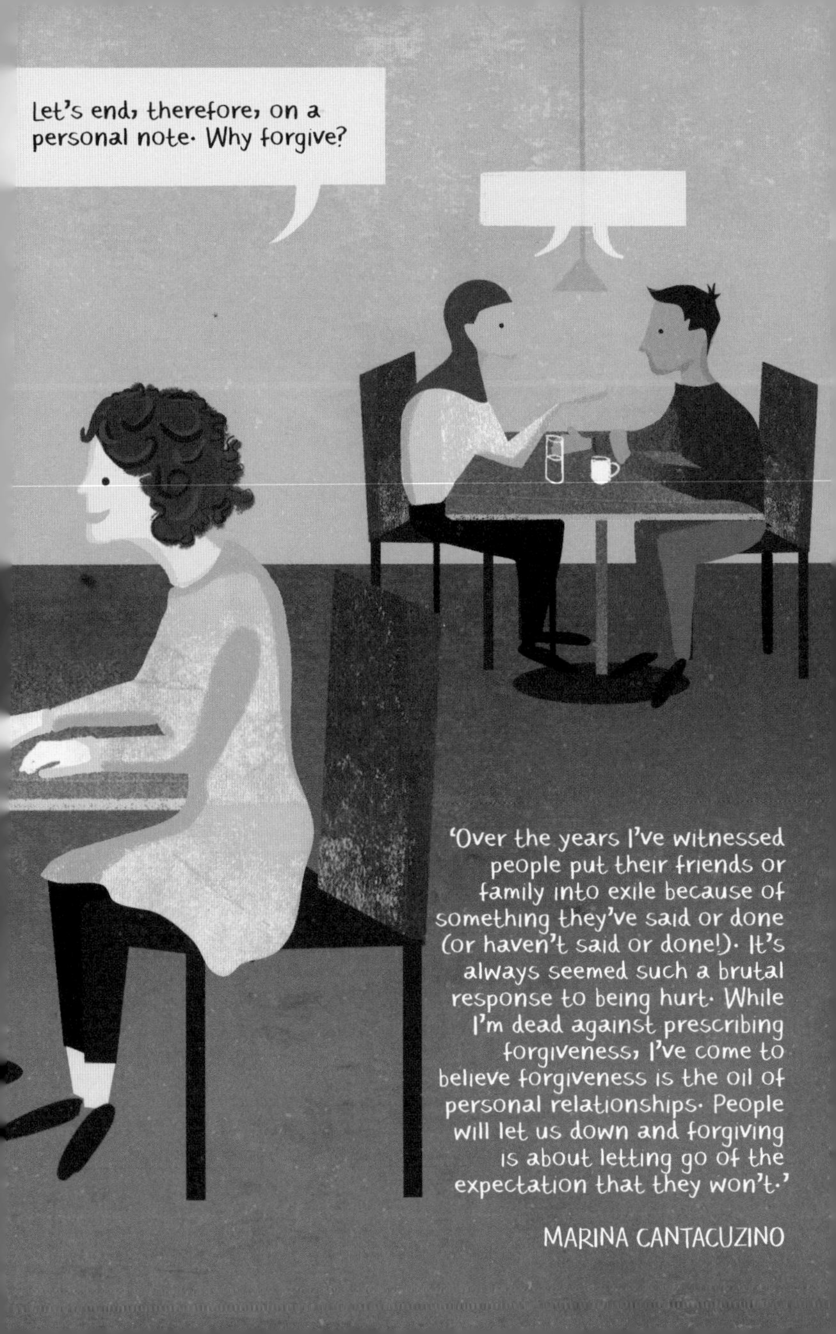
Let's end, therefore, on a personal note. Why forgive?
'Over the years I've witnessed people put their friends or family into exile because of something they've said or done (or haven't said or done!). It's always seemed such a brutal response to being hurt. While I'm dead against prescribing forgiveness, I've come to believe forgiveness is the oil of personal relationships. People will let us down and forgiving is about letting go of the expectation that they won't.'
MARINA CANTACUZINO

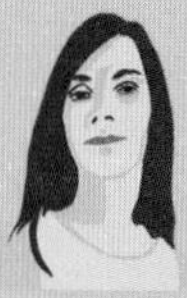
Madeleine Black

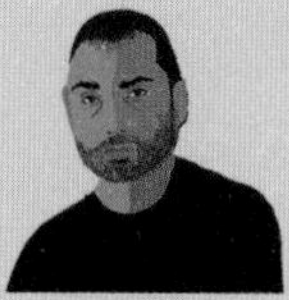
Pardeep Kaleka

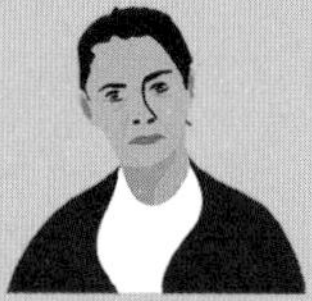
Robi Damelin

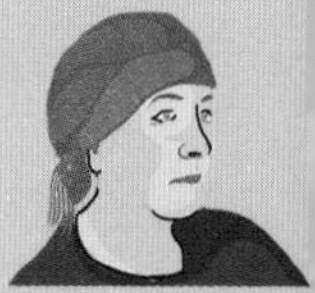
Kelly Connor

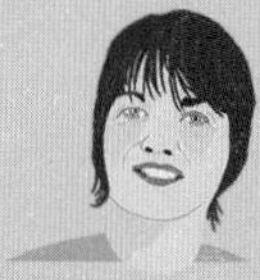
Anne Gallagher

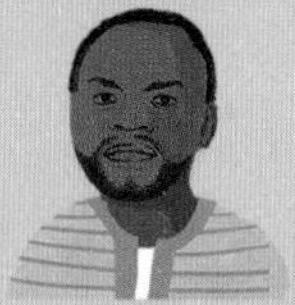
Letlapa Mphahlele

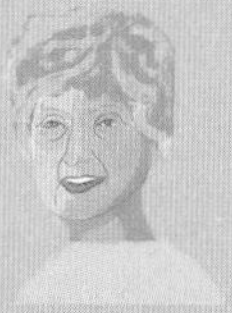
Eva Kor

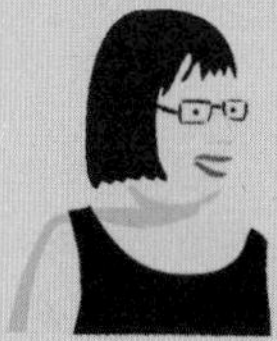
Ginn Fourie

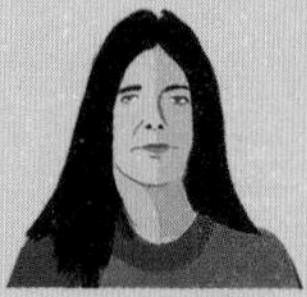
Jo Berry

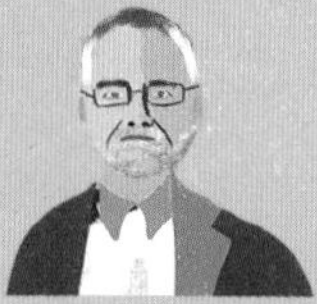
Patrick Magee

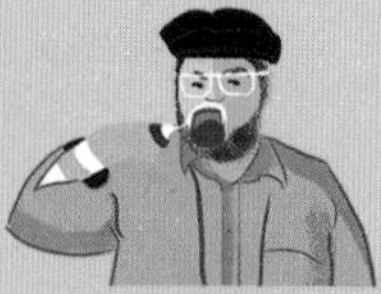
Michael Lapsley

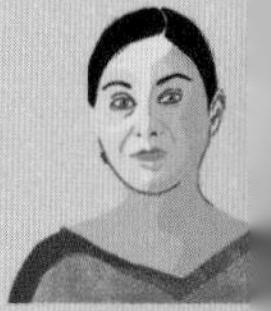
Gill Hicks

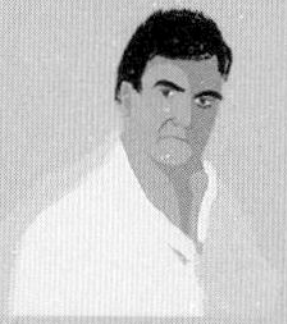
Rami Elhanan

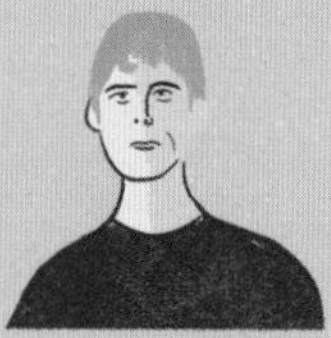
Arno Michaelis

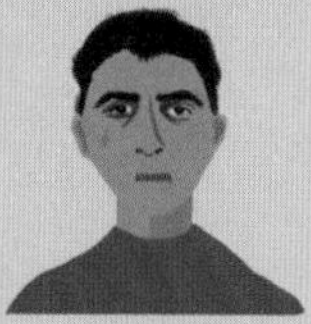
Bassam Aramin

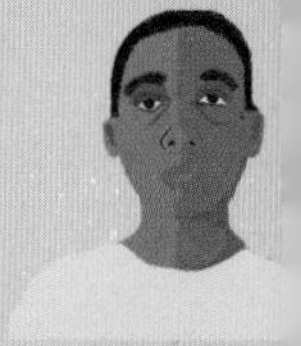
Shad Ali

The story-tellers who have generously shared their stories with The Forgiveness Project (www.theforgivenessproject.com)

For references to specific research studies and individual
stories cited in this book, please see
www.singingdragon.com/catalogue/book/9781785921247

Copyright © The Forgiveness Project and Masi Noor 2018
Illustrations copyright © Sophie Standing 2018

This is a first edition.

Published by Singing Dragon
an imprint of Jessica Kingsley Publishers
73 Collier Street
London N1 9BE, UK
and
400 Market Street, Suite 400
Philadelphia, PA 19106, USA

www.singingdragon.com

ISBN 978 1 78592 124 7
eISBN 978 0 85701 279 1

Printed and bound in China

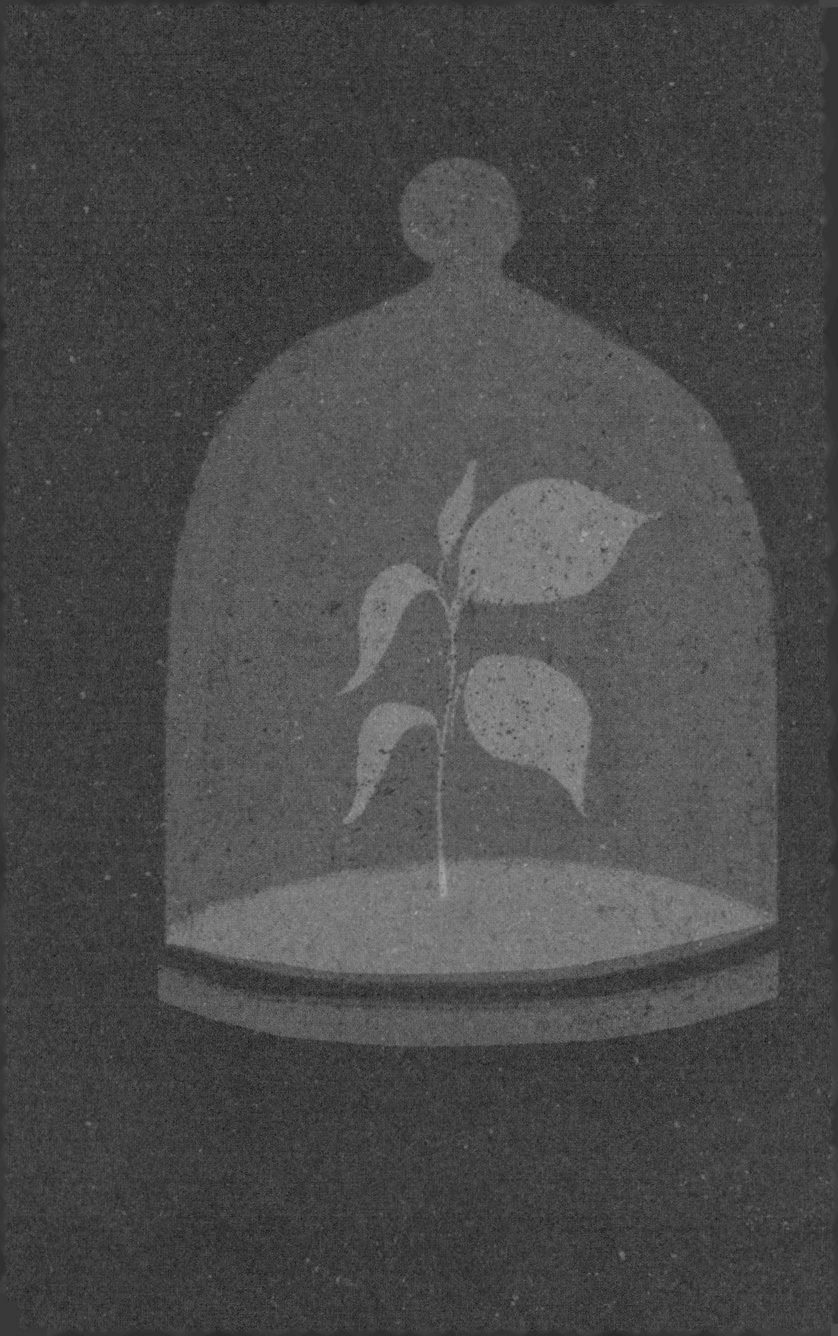